Debates on Colonial Genocide in the 21st Century

Marouf Hasian, Jr.

Debates on Colonial Genocide in the 21st Century

palgrave
macmillan

Marouf Hasian, Jr.
University of Utah
Salt Lake City, UT, USA

ISBN 978-3-030-21277-3 ISBN 978-3-030-21278-0 (eBook)
https://doi.org/10.1007/978-3-030-21278-0

This Palgrave Pivot imprint is published by the registered company Springer Nature Switzerland AG
The registered company address is: Gewerbestrasse 11, 6330 Cham, Switzerland

Acknowledgments

I have spent years mulling over many of the ideas that appear in this book, and I want to begin by thanking my father, Marouf Hasian, Sr., who passed away before he had a chance to read some of my work on the Nakba. For many years I was allowed to travel with him on his road trips, and I heard countless coffee shop discussions among Palestinians of all ages who were living in the diaspora. They worked in places like Charlotte or St. Louis or Kenosha or Detroit or New York but they yearned for a time when they could return to an independent Palestinian state. My father and I used to joke about how this same exact military post that was in his village was once occupied at different historical points in time by Ottoman, British, Jordanian, and Israeli forces. Little did I know that as I listened to stories like this those memories would help me understand what scholars meant when they wrote about how Al-Nakba involved ongoing structural processes and not simply a single event.

I would also like to thank the undergraduate students at the University of Utah who have taken my classes on the documentation of genocides. Over the last decade, whenever I got the chance to teach that class I updated the materials, and as I collected various case study materials, I realized that I needed to write a short book on colonial genocide debates.

I was able to finish writing several drafts of this book while I was on sabbatical during the fall of 2018, but as the Chair of the Department of Communication, Danielle Endres, can attest, it was a very strange sabbatical semester filled with a number of challenges. For many years, even before she became chair, she has been one of my strongest supporters, and I want to thank her, as well as Professor Kent Ono, for keeping me on task.

The Dean of our College of Humanities here at the University of Utah, Stuart Culver, continues to provide me with the time and support that I have needed as I worked on manuscripts like this.

I would like to thank two folks who work with the Pivot series at Palgrave who had faith in my work and helped immensely—Michelle Chen and Alina Yurova. Each of them, in their own ways, provided needed encouragement at various stages of the publication process.

Last, but not least, I want to thank the various external reviewers who provided very detailed suggestions about how to strengthen this Pivot book.

Contents

CHAPTER 1

Introduction: Critical Genocide Studies and the Need for Twenty-First-Century Decolonization Debates

Abstract In this particular chapter the author explains how critical genocide studies differ from traditional Holocaust analyses or orthodox social scientific studies of "modern" genocides. The author contends that twenty-first-century scholars and public care very deeply about apologies, expressions of regret, the repatriation of remains, and reparations for colonial wrongdoing, and that we need more nuanced "decolonizing" debates about these topics. This chapter also helps explain some of the reluctance of former colonial-settler states to revisit these postcolonial topics that oftentimes ask nation-states to "master" their fraught imperial or colonial pasts in the same way that Germany was once asked to "master" Nazi pasts. Portions of this chapter also defend the heuristic value of critical genealogical and critical genocide studies approaches to genocide disputation.

Keywords Critical genocide studies • Holocaust • Palestine • Reparations • Settler colonialism • Tasmania

The scholarly and public recognition of any genocide, including the Holocaust, depends on the confluence of a host of factors and should be viewed as a rhetorical and argumentative achievement. Raul Hilberg, who wrote one of the most famous books that outlined some of the major features of the Nazi machinery that was responsible for the perpetration of

M. Hasian, Jr., *Debates on Colonial Genocide in the 21st Century*,
https://doi.org/10.1007/978-3-030-21278-0_1

ethnic cleansing of Jews,[1] tells the story of how post-World War II publishers were reluctant to publish a book that went beyond recognition of concentration camps in analyses of death camps.[2] Norman Finkelstein tried to explain some of the politics behind this reluctance:

> It is hard now to remember that the Nazi holocaust was once a taboo subject. During the early years of the Cold War, mention of the Nazi holocaust was seen as undermining the critical U.S.-West German alliance. It was airing the dirty laundry of the barely de-Nazified West German elites and thereby playing into the hands of the Soviet Union, which didn't tire of remembering the crimes of the West German "revanchists."[3]

Cold War politics thus influenced both the scholarly and public reception of some Holocaust research.

Before journalists traveled to Jerusalem to cover the Adolph Eichmann trial, few communities knew very much about the Judeocide.[4] There was a deal of confusion about what happened in both the Nazi concentration camps as well as the death camps. Thanks to survivor testimony, the interrogation of massive numbers of German documents for Nuremberg prosecutions, and the curatorial efforts of those who assemble museological displays at places like the United States Holocaust Memorial Museum (USHMM) we have learned a great deal. We have also learned how millions of global denizens can combat all types of Holocaust denialism. Thanks to these consciousness-raising efforts Auschwitz, Treblinka, or Sobibór are now recognizable names that appear in canonical academic Holocaust texts and in vernacular commentaries.

That said, some of the same community members who have applauded this Holocaust-consciousness-raising have oftentimes been circumspect in the ways that they evaluate calls for inclusion of other mass murders in the pantheon of acceptable genocides. As Alexander Hinton would note in 2017, critical genealogical studies of Holocaust scholarship and genocide studies would show that they had been "informed by an implicit canon and prioritization of cases, led by the Holocaust prototype and an exemplary triad consisting of the Armenian genocide, Holocaust, and Rwandan genocide."[5] Hinton elaborated by noting that some gatekeepers wanted to make sure that only a few genocides could meet the high standards set by that triad of historical incidents.

It would be a mistake, however, to think that only scholars want to place restrictions on the usage of genocidal labels. This is not some example of "mere rhetoric" where grammatological choices are inconsequential. The political fallout that came from belated interventionism in Srebrenica[6] or Rwanda[7] underscored the point that labeling of large-scale massacres as a "genocide"—the "g word"—carried weight and triggered potential legal, economic, social, and political repercussions.[8]

Interest in expanding the number of genocides—to include more "modern" genocides (like what is happening to the Rohingya in Myanmar)[9] or "colonial genocides" (like the Ovaherero and Nama genocide in "German South West Africa")[10]—waxes and wanes, depending on a number of factors, including the number of stakeholders, access to international presses, the historical sensibilities of audiences, the contours of public memories, and the presentist needs of communities.[11]

In March 2019, some readers of global news outlets were shocked to read that Mexico's president, Andrés Manuel López Obrador, was demanding that Spain and the Vatican apologize for the violent conquest of Mexico.[12] Mexico's first leftist president in some seven decades has previously talked about reducing inequities in Mexico and helping combat poverty, and now President Obrador was tweeting out video addresses from archaeological sites as he explained to viewers that he wanted Felipe VI of Spain to acknowledge and apologize for the atrocities that were committed against "indigenous peoples for the violations of what we now call human rights."[13] Reconciliation was important, noted Obrador, but before that time the former conquerors needed to admit that the sword and the cross were used commit reprehensible colonial acts that warranted public acknowledgments and apologies. Spanish governmental officials in Madrid quickly rejected President Obrador's request, and they publicized a text that indicated that the "arrival, 500 years ago, of Spaniards to present Mexican territory cannot be judged in light of contemporary considerations."[14]

Was Obrador implying that Spanish conquerors had once carried out a "genocide" in this part of the world? Was Mexico's president basing his arguments on scholarly research on these topics, or was his commentary directed at national or international audiences who might share some of his postcolonial views? It is telling that in a public survey that was conducted by the Center for Sociological Research in 1992, it was found that some 33 percent of those Spaniards surveyed indicated that they were "proud" of the Spanish conquest of America while only 5 percent mentioned any "genocide."[15] One Spanish lawmaker tweeted during the spring of 2019 that the Spaniards "went there and finished with the power of tribes who assassinated their neighbors cruelly and viciously," and that was the reason why just a few Spanish warriors "conquered and civilized that land."[16] Spain's Foreign Minister, Josep Borrell, noted that Spain would not offer any "extemporaneous apologies" to Mexico, and he elaborated by arguing that his nation had no interest in asking the French Republic for an apology for what Napoleon's soldiers did when they invaded Spain. Borrell was fairly sure that the French were not going to demand "an apology from the Italians for Julius Caesar's conquest of Gaul."[17]

All sorts of moral equivalence arguments were being made in these contentious disputes over colonial wrongdoing and potential postcolonial apologies.[18]

Depending on the criteria that these arguers use, the availability of evidence, disciplinary expectations, and other rhetorical factors, scholars or members of public who write about colonial atrocities or imperial genocides can either contract, or they can expand, the list of administrative mass murders or ethnic cleansings that deserve to be called "genocides." Is it possible that many twenty-first-century scholars and audiences are willing to use the term "genocide" when they talk about happened during the twentieth century in places like Armenia or Rwanda or Srebrenica but are unwilling to use that phrase in disputation over conquests that happened 500 years ago? How much time must have passed, and what other factors help influence the ways that academics, journalists, laypersons, and others converse about these topics?

In this particular book I join Alexander Hinton, A. Dirk Moses, and other critical genocide scholars who argue that it is time that Holocaust scholars and postcolonial critics start talking to each other as they revisit the question of how twenty-first-century social agents should define, describe, and explain everything from the causes of genocides to genocidal prevention. In place of more restrictive ways of defining genocide—that are often based on narrow interpretations of the work of Raphaël Lemkin[19]—I will be advocating that researchers *operationally define genocides* in more expansive ways by paying more attention to the structural, functional, or material features of large-scale massacres. Moreover, I will be arguing that members of the public and many others should be involved in the process of determining when genocides will be acknowledged and when interventions are needed to help with the pursuit of post-conflict restorative justice.

These dialogues about the expansion of the number of acknowledged genocides should be carried out in many different venues. Decision-makers, researchers, diplomats, and others should risk opening up what scholars and investigative journalists call the "Pandora's Box" that might lead to many future requests for official apologies or the filing of many (post)colonial lawsuits.[20]

I believe in the need for more debates about the revisionist labeling of colonial atrocities because genocides are not simply events but structures and processes as well.[21] The Armenian genocide was carried out in several phases,[22] and it could be argued that Ottoman militarists and other imperialists carried out similar genocidal attacks on Greeks and other communities.[23] The few dozen Nazi leaders who met at the Wannsee Conference were only some of those who were "Hitler's Willing Executioners,"[24] and writers like Timothy Snyder remind us that Stalin and Hitler received a great deal of help when they, and their minions, were carrying out atrocities in the "Bloodlands."[25] Countless soldiers and collaborators were involved in the perpetration of genocidal acts during World War II, and more than a few knew about the horrors of the death squads, the gas chambers in the death camps, and the forced marches near the end of the war.

As some researchers are now arguing, it may be possible that several different genocides were being carried out throughout World War II,[26] and a host of racist, militaristic, gendered,[27] and nationalistic ideologies may have motivated both the oppressors and the oppressed when they participated in all of this carnage.[28] In the same ways that Holocaust researchers are now complicating the ways that we critique Eastern European representations of the Shoah[29] scholars who look back at colonial genocides use comparative approaches as they note how several empires were involved in the perpetration of atrocities.[30] A whole host of intentionalist,[31] functionalist,[32] or structuralist approaches are now employed in the carrying out of twenty-first-century investigations of those colonial genocides.[33]

In some historical situations transcontinental observers who watched what was happening on the peripheries of empire complained about the commission of "atrocities" or the "extirpation" of the "Aborigines,"[34] while at other times other names for these mass murders would be used by earlier generations who wondered about the wisdom of settler colonial exterminationist practices.[35]

In many ways there are scholarly clues that these multifaceted debates about colonial genocides are once again in the news, fueled by academic or public disputation about whether we should only use definitions of genocide that allow reviewers to show the "intentional destruction" of an ethnic group, in part or in whole in "physical" or "biological" ways.[36] Others are equally convinced that participants in these definitional disputes ought to include "cultural" definitions of genocide as well.[37]

Oftentimes academics indicate whether they want to see expansive or restrictive interpretations of genocidal guidelines. Some scholars, like Güenter Lewy, are known for using the work of Raphaël Lemkin in restrictive ways, and it is said that Lewy is one of those researchers who has had qualms about including the Armenian genocide in that list of canonical events that Professor Hinton referenced. Using narrow interpretations of the UN's adoption of Lemkin's definitions of genocide Lewy defends the position that few events, outside the World War II Holocaust, deserve to be treated as genuine genocides.[38]

Other writers, like Norbert Finzsch, have a very different take on this definitional labor, and they do not mind including other genocidal studies in the formation of new canons. Professor Finzsch seems to be bothered by some of the usages of legalistic criteria that restrict the number of recognizable genocides, and he has argued that if "it looks luck a duck, if it walks like a duck, if it quacks like a duck," then it must be a duck. Norbert Finzsch is averring that there are differences between the acknowledgments of the ontological existence of genocides and *the epistemic labelling of those events.*[39]

Although those researchers who want to patrol the canons and restrict the number of genocides may outnumber those who want to see "critical" revisionism, there are vocal academics who make some convincing arguments about how Holocaust scholars and indigenous writers need to talk with each other instead of ignoring each other's work. A. Dirk Moses wants to move beyond Auschwitz-centered, legalistic ways of defining genocides, and he opined that the UN Convention on Genocide's adoption of some of Raphaël Lemkin's work ought to be treated as a "political-juridical instrument" and not some "timeless" agreement that was "beyond the realm of politics."[40] He noted that the reluctance to expand the canons of traditional genocides involved a "conceptual blockage" or a "definitional dilemma" that stemmed, in large part, from genocidal definitions that were based on a "prototype," a "paradigmatic genocide" that underlies "the normative definition against which all others are measured."[41] He went on to claim that some settler colonial genocides, and other historical "atrocities" may not fit that proto-typical Auschwitz-centered way of categorizing intentional large-scale mass murders.[42]

Professor Moses wanted to see some indigenous types of colonial acts of mass violence treated as genocides, even if they did not resemble the pictures that some had of Auschwitz gas chambers or mobile killing machines.[43]

Other authors may be interested in defending the formalistic criteria for genocides that I mentioned above, which come from experts like Lemkin, or they may want to defend the conventional ways that scholars, politicians, and laypersons talk and write about the Holocaust or the genocide, but I respectfully disagree. I will be using several cases studies in this book to defend the argument that all decision-makers and global denizens need to *treat genocidal recognition as a rhetorical achievement*. By this, I mean that deciding whether to include a particular colonial "atrocity" or ethnic cleansing of civilians during imperial expansionist years in the traditional pantheon of genocides is not something that can, or should, be determined solely by single authors or small groups of academics. These researchers should not be allowed to police and to cordon off genocidal claims that come from activists and others who are asking for genocidal revisionism. Nor should those decisions be made based on post-World War II definitions of genocide that were intended to deflect attention away from the potential genocidal acts that were committed by American, British, French, Russian, and other victors after World War II.[44]

If this means that we have to acknowledge the commission of dozens of colonial genocides over the course of hundreds of years of imperial expansionism by diverse imperialists, then so be it.[45] That would be better than pretending that genocidal acts were not perpetrated during colonial periods, where deceptive archives are co-produced by those who wish to believe that benevolent colonizers did their best to peacefully carry out their civilization missions.[46] It would also be better than pretending that only totalitarian governments are involved in the perpetration of genocides.[47]

In this book I extend the work of critical genealogists,[48] critical genocide scholars, settler colonial theorists, postcolonial critics, and others who are adamant that publics and activists should have some say in resolving some of these genocidal issues. Historical and current events in places like Canada, Germany, Israel, Namibia, and Tasmania show that the decision to recognize, or to not recognize, historical colonial events as genocidal in nature can impact everything from the tearing down of statues[49] to the paying of reparations to the recharacterization of imperial archives. This is especially the case when those who want to make decisions regarding the inclusion or exclusion of particular colonial practices as genocides are living in former settler colonies, where observers have to witness "ideological slights of hand," the formation of "many layers of psychosocial denial and contradiction," and calls for acknowledgments that are "fraught with anxiety and guilt."[50]

Although there are many different dimensions of what I have elsewhere called the "Indigeneity wars,"[51] in this particular Pivot book I want to focus in on the scholarly and public dimensions of disputation over the potential inclusion of controversial "colonial" or "settler-colonial" abuses that might warrant characterizations as indigenocides[52] or genocides.

As I explain in more detail below, the case studies that I have chosen have been selected because these are cases where large communities of indigenous communities, vocal activists, or others involved in "decolonization" practices have demanded that some colonial events or imperial "atrocity" decisions be viewed in the same ways that Europeans and others view the Holocaust or the Rwanda genocides.

With this in mind, let me briefly explain why I have chosen the two main case studies that provide some of the major scaffolding for this book.

Why These Particular Case Studies?

The two case studies that serve as the focal points for my claims—the Tasmanian genocide and the Nakba—involve situations where empowered decisions-makers ***are reluctant to call some historical incidents colonial genocides.*** In each of these two situations there have been groups of activists, or dissident scholars, who have asked that these large-scale massacres be treated as a type of "indigenocide" or "genocide," but in each case researchers, descendants of settler colonial communities, or other groups have refused to characterized these colonial or imperial events as genocidal in nature.[53]

Take for example, the Tasmanian situation that will serve as the first case study in this book. The Tasmanian Aborigines have oftentimes been treated as communities who either "disappeared" from the face of the earth in 1876—with the recorded death of the Bruny Islander/Palawa Truganini—or as an ethnic group that was almost wiped out by British colonization.[54] For almost a decade during the first quarter of the nineteenth century the Tasmanians fought against the British soldiers, convicts, and local collaborators who tried to wipe them out during what would be called the "Black Wars." Using a variety of confrontational, segregationist, conciliatory, and annihilationist discourses supporters of British expansionism could rationalize their treatment of the Aboriginal "other." They could rationalize the sheep production, the farming, and the settlement of "Van Diemen's Land" (later called Tasmania) at the same time that they characterized anti-Aboriginal violence as necessitous colonial warfare. Several generations of colonial settlers would use Social Darwinian, eugenical, anthropological, and other arguments to assert that the Tasmanians were a dying race, and that settlers had an obligation to turn supposedly uninhabited lands (*terra nullius*) into productive colonies.

The remnants of the Tasmanians were first moved to Flinders Island, and then to Oyster Cove the following decade.[55] By this time only a few dozen Tasmanians were said to be alive, and European researchers and others flocked to Tasmania so that they could conduct investigations before the "passing" of this supposedly exotic "race."

When Tasmanian activists and others later wrote about all of this colonial settler violence—and characterized it as "genocidal" in nature—this created all types of scholarly and public firestorms. Some alleged that disease and indigenous in-fighting is what caused the demise of the Tasmanians, while others argued that the "Black War" was fought between equally powerful warring communities. More than a few argued that those in London or Hobart did their best to help save, not "extirpate" the Tasmanians, and that all of this benevolence provided historical evidence that could be used to refute allegations that any of this constituted any "intentional" genocide.

In some cases—as I note in the next chapter—academics demanded that before activists and scholars label this a "Tasmanian genocide" they actually count the number of Tasmanian dead during the 1820s and 1830s before rendering historical or legal judgment.

In sum, both the select histories that chronicled these settler colonial acts, as well as the public memories of these archival histories, became contested terrains for disputation that can lead to denialism or revisionism as various observers comment on the heritage rights of more than 23,000 Tasmanians.[56] It is no coincidence that some researchers have trouble framing these settler colonial affairs in the same ways that they configure what happened during the "true" genocides like the Armenian or Rwandan genocides.

In the case of the Nakba we are dealing with a situation where, until recently, there were few researchers in the West who even considered including this potential "catastrophe" in any anthology of works of the Holocaust or genocides. While a few Israel groups, including Zochrot, a non-profit organization, take visitors on Nakba tours,[57] other Israelis worry that al-Nakba consciousness-raising threatens state legitimacy. When most Western audiences think of the uprooting of 700,000 Palestinians they think of disputes over "refugee" status, not genocidal argumentation. Instead of viewing this as some "ethnic cleansing" or the intentional carrying out of any physical, biological, or cultural genocide many Israeli supporters argue that in 1948 global communities witnessed the spontaneous Arab Palestinian fleeing that was based on calls from neighboring Arab nations.

The chapter on the Nakba in this book provides a detailed critical analysis of some of these academic and journalistic debates so that readers can decide whether they are willing to think about revising the genocidal canons to include the Nakba.

Given all of this contestation in Tasmanian and Palestinian contexts, it makes sense that researchers interested in these heated conversations look for analytic frameworks that allow them to interrogate both academic and public argumentation.

The Heuristic Value of Critical Genealogical and Critical Genocide Studies Approaches to Genocide Disputation

Although there are a number of fruitful ways that one might go about studying colonial "extirpation" or imperial "atrocities," this particular book will use critical genealogical methods and other "critical" approaches to get at the discourse/power/knowledge dynamics of all of this genocidal disputation.[58] Unlike other books that oftentimes begin by citing the definition of "genocide" that comes from supporters of Raphaël Lemkin or the United Nations Genocide Convention, this is a book that places the work of writers like Lemkin *in conversation with many other social agents.* This is a book that is more interested in functional and structural ways of conceptualizing genocides that do not ask researchers to look for those "smoking guns" that might come from the intentionalist studies of the words and deeds of single individuals who may be accused of carrying out a genocide.[59]

This more rhetorical way of thinking about genocides *is audience centered*, and it highlights the importance of public debate and argumentation in scholarly and public contexts. It pays attention to the ways that genocide survivors, or the generations of descendants of those who suffered from colonial horrors, have argued about indigenocides or genocides. In other words, this is a book that will be using the Tasmanian and Nakba cases as examples of both scholarly and vernacular disputation, which puts on display how various audiences in public spheres win or lose arguments about genocidal status.

Sadly, I will also be noting that the "decolonizing" of some conventional ways of arguing about genocides shows that there are also times when some empowered officials in nation-states appropriate the language of "cultural genocide" as a way of *closing off debates* about frontier settler violence. Apologies or expressions of regret can take the place of payment of reparations or the redistribution of lands that were occupied by colonizers, and some crafty decision-makers do their best to avoid discussing "physical" or "biological" genocide in their own colonial histories or imperial legacies. At other times, what initially looks an official apology can quickly turn into a eulogistic way of speaking about some nation's frontier or settler past.[60]

Again, I recognize that these are contestable claims. What members of former settler colonial communities, after all, want to have their children visit museums so that they can learn about starvation on the plains,[61] forced migrations, the lack of enforcement of old treaties, the placement of indigenous peoples on "reservations" or refugee camps, or the perpetration of other reprehensible acts?

Drawing from the work of writers like Michel Foucault, Ann Stoler,[62] Edward Said,[63] Judith Butler,[64] and many other critical scholars, I will be arguing that investigators and readers need to pay attention to longitudinal ways that particular "genealogies" (Foucault) are produced by both winners and losers in representational contests over the rhetorical framing of some major "extirpation," "atrocity," or "genocide."

Like many influential critical theorists Michel Foucault bequeathed to us many essays and books that provide hints of how he thought that critical scholars needed to go about producing those counterhistories, the counter-memories, or other texts that could be used by the disempowered and others to counter the discursive influence of what he called a hegemonic "*dispositif*."[65] I contend that the constitutive imperial formation, and the colonial (mis)recognition, of various confrontational, segregationist, annihilationist, and conciliatory rhetorical acts, helped build and maintain dense colonial knowledge assemblages.[66]

Foucault is oftentimes remembered as someone who wants to theorize about how various critical genealogical critiques might disrupted taken-for-granted power structures. According to Foucault, scholars who studied societal contests were supposed to look for "manifold relations of power which permeate, characterize and constitute the social body, and these relations of power cannot themselves be established, consolidated nor implemented without the production, accumulation, circulation and functioning of a discourse."[67] This is why researchers today often comment on his defense of the troika, discourse/power/knowledge.

Researchers who identified these large, and influential, discursive formations were then supposed to take the next perspectival step, and begin identifying and tracing the smaller fragments ("elements," *epistemes*) that went into the crafting of these larger, contested discursive formations. When these elements or *epistemes* coalesced in key social, economic, legal, or cultural contexts they could form some massive, and hegemonic "*dispositif*." Overtime some ideological formations became so accepted and so naturalized that future generations conveniently forgot their rhetorical or historical origins and treated them as essentialized "truths."

Drawing from the work of Friedrich Nietzsche, Foucault at times wrote about the use and abuse of histories, and the "grey" nature of the "parchment" that went into all types of archives.[68] At the same time that he asked his followers to study "truth effects" in place of essentialist "truths" Foucault outlined some factors that might need to be kept in mind as critical investigators tracked the evolution and movement of some of these *epistemes* or elements. In his lecture, "The Discourse on Language," Foucault noted how "a series of discourses are formed, through, in spite of, or with, the aid of these systems of restraint," and he invited critics to note "what were the specific norms for each, and what were the conditions of appearance, growth, and variation."[69] For Foucault, the discourse/power/knowledge that was co-produced by the empowered in places like prisons or mental facilities did not simply depend on the use of raw physical power, but the creation, and the public acceptance, of governmental mentalities, apparatus, and other accoutrements of disciplinary power.[70]

Critical scholars have expressed an interest in applying Foucauldian concepts in colonial settlement contexts,[71] and Foucault once argued that researchers need to interrogate the "myriad disciplining strategies" that were adopted from European "institutional life"—the military barracks, the workplaces, the monasteries, and so on.[72] Those who advocate taking this approach could then study the polysemic (multiple meanings) or the polyvalent (multiple values) associated with hegemonic colonial structures and mentalities. These formations, for example, could be treated as "entanglements of varied spatialities and techniques."[73]

To provide readers with just one example of how researchers might apply Foucauldian ways of treating rhetorics in colonial or postcolonial situations, note the ways that critical investigators might trace the lingering power of the antecedent colonial genres that are a part of today's (post)colonial conversations about "reconciliation." As Stephen Winter once noted, part of the reason for the contested nature of the term "reconciliation" has to do with some of its religious etymology, what Winter characterized as its "radical polysemy."[74]

The ideograph "reconciliation" also has more secular and *realpolitik* genealogies, and there are ideological reasons for the continued resonance of that term. During the early nineteenth century many Europeans, influenced by debates about transcontinental slave trades and slave emancipation, used the term "conciliation" when they wanted to reference non-violent ways of negotiating with Aboriginal communities in places like Tasmania, Australia, or Canada. This allowed European interventionists in indigenous affairs—who were ashamed of the "annihilationist" rhetorics that were circulated by violent settlers, convicts, and others—to argue that beneficent colonialism was to be preferred over more barbaric ways of configuring frontier violence.

Lingering rhetorical traces of these older settler colonial phrases can be found in twenty-first-century "truth and reconciliation" efforts that oftentimes end up, ironically, being used by those who wish to critique some of the discourses that were produced by historical British, Australian, or Tasmanian conciliators.

Foucauldians who are interested in critical genocide studies might begin any comparative studies of cases like the Tasmanian genocide or the Nakba by noting the structural or functional relationships that existed between at least three epistemic clusters of settler colonial rhetorics:

1. Calls for the outright "extirpation" or annihilation of indigenous cultures. Examples of this would appear in some of the rhetorics that would be used in the destruction of indigenous communities in California,[75] Tasmania, or German South West Africa, where, instead of needing the labor of those who were colonized violent colonizers

simply asserted that they needed the "blacks" "extirpation." Either Whites provided the labor or colonial settlers could support the migration of "colored" laborers from other colonies.

Twenty-first century interdisciplinary scholars use the terms "biological" and "physical" genocide when they are referring to what the "conciliators" once called the "extirpation" of the "aborigines."

2. Sometimes those living in metropoles or the peripheries of empires used combinations of annihilationist and insidious variants of assimilation rhetorics. For example, some colonial administrators and soldiers claimed that they had tried, and failed, to reason with warlike indigenous communities and had to resort to the use of force. "Native" recalcitrance led to "rebellion" and the "necessity" of using overwhelming force. In theory, the violent nature of barbarian "others" had forced the hand of colonial setters who would have preferred to support segregationist or assimilationist policies.
3. At the other end of the discursive spectrum that I have outlined one would find examples of demands for the total assimilation of indigenous communities. Sometimes members of colonial or imperial societies used variants of these assimilationist rhetorics when they wanted to rationalize policies like the ones that led to the "stolen generations" of Australian Aboriginal children and Torres Islander children who were removed from their families by church groups, state government agencies, or the Australian Federal government.[76] Here, distinctions were made between those who could be assimilated and those who could not be assimilated. Lorenzo Veracini quoted the infamous words of the American Richard Pratt, who suggested that pioneers and their supporters who came across those who could be saved needed to "kill the Indian in him and save the man."[77]

Lives could be saved, but cultures might be lost.

Scholars and lay persons, using consequentialist ways of conceptualizing these activities, may view these segregationist or assimilationist efforts as destructive activities, but those living in former settler communities could respond that the "intent" here was innocent, reformist, or rehabilitative. The adoption of assimilationist or accommodationist ways of viewing settler-Aboriginal relationships could be configured as a constructive alternative to the annihilationist rhetorics of those who simply wanted to wipe out the "blacks" or other indigenous communities.

> Savior rhetorics are crafted by those who can reconfigure these segregationist or assimilations discursive elements, and permutations of these arguments oftentimes reappeared in the guise of presentist advocacy for the recognition of "cultural genocides."

As Foucault and others have noted, over time we forget about the motives of those who produced these types of governmental rhetorics, and in the case of debates about colonial genocides the presence or absence of materials in the "archives" influences the trajectory of scholarly or public argumentation.

Foucauldians, who care about the power of those who produce histories and counterhistories, memories and countermemories, treat the archives as heterotopic places of colonial knowledge production and contestation. These are not necessarily spaces and places for revealing preexisting "truths" about genocidal practices, but are colonial archival places of epistemic production that are visited by those who want to find out, or evaluate, what happened in "1948." As various Palestinian or Israeli communities argue over whether this was a "catastrophe" or a war of independence for the survival of those in the Yishuv these communities are not simply performing revelatory acts of fact discovery but are also engaged in fact production—something that Foucault characterized as "truth effects."

In settler-colonial contexts this impacts how we view talk of "conciliation" and "reconciliation." There are simply times when rhetorics of conciliation end up being used to aid the cause of those interested in legitimating frontier expansionism. This is one of the reasons why Hannah Wylie would write in 2017 that in order to understand the theoretical and practical dimensions of post-conflict genocidal debates we need "additional research on how a genealogy of reconciliation" might inform the ways that Canadian scholars and citizens deal with invocations of that term.[78]

Scholars and readers may disagree about whether the growing recognition of "cultural genocide" in Canadian contexts opens, or closes, doors for other critiques, but there is little question that some researchers firmly believe we have to pay attention to the power/discourse/knowledge dynamics of these situations. As Pamela Palmater has recently noted:

> Part of the decolonization process for Indigenous and non-Indigenous peoples alike is to acknowledge the history of Canada—both the feel-good sentiments about peace and friendship and the darker side of the colonization

> process, which continues into the present day. This acknowledgment includes recognizing how we define, interpret, and apply both the law of genocide and the punishment for it.[79]

The same type of analysis, I contend, should inform the ways that we approach the Tasmanian and Nakba cases.

Conclusion

It is understandable that some readers may disagree about whether the case studies that I have chosen are really instances of indigenocide or genocide, but the point of this Pivot book is to show that the patrolling of genocidal boundaries is a matter of politics and ideological contestation. It is not simply a matter of deductively finding the best definition for genocide and then applying that definition to cases of settler colonial or Aboriginal violence.

I dare say that if readers today approached some of the same well-known Holocaust and genocide experts, and if they asked those groups of experts to draw up a list of the dozen or so recognizable genocides, few of those lists would contain the exact same numbers of genocides. Some, using Auschwitz-type criteria, may argue that only the Holocaust actually qualifies as a genocide,[80] and others might also name the Armenian or the Cambodian or the Rwandan genocide. After invoking those few names, notice how opinions start to diverge when it comes to the inclusion of other potential genocides.

If this is the case, then interdisciplinary scholars who study these debates, as well as global citizens, need to pay attention to the genealogical histories behind these various colonial debates as well as the politics behind what Derek Gregory calls the "colonial present."[81] Presentist needs, and the absence or presence of public pressures and political will, oftentimes influence whether a particular large-scale massacre will be treated as another "forgotten" genocide.

I am convinced that only by moving away from conventional, deductive analyses that depend on Lemkin-like frames can we get at the politics and the power that helps explain the reticence of many to include colonial genocides in the "canons" of "real" genocides. Andrew Woolford and James Gacek, writing in 2017, argued that the use of Foucauldian approaches can aid those who are interested in unpacking some of the ideologies and the structural processes that were involved in settler colonial destruction and what they call "genocidal carcerality."[82]

I would extend those insights and argue that twenty-first-century audiences—living in ages filled with apologies and talk of reconciliation—may soon be faced with more adamant demands for payment of reparations, the repatriation of human remains, and the redistribution of "stolen" lands. Studying the cases in this book provides an excellent way of beginning the process of understanding the complexities of these colonial and (post)colonial genocidal situations.

Notes

1. Raul Hilberg, *The Destruction of the European Jews* (1961; New York: Holmes & Meier, 1985). For an excellent overview of some of the issues that Hilberg had to deal with, see David S. Wyman, "Managing the Death Machine," *The New York Times*, last modified August 11, 1985, https://www.nytimes.com/1985/08/11/books/managing-the-death-machine.html
2. See Raul Hilberg, *The Politics of Memory: The Journey of a Holocaust Historian* (Chicago: Ivan R. Dee, 1996).
3. Norman Finkelstein, "Remembering Raul Hilberg," *Counterpunch*, paragraph 5, last modified August 22, 2007, https://www.counterpunch.org/2007/08/22/remembering-raul-hilberg/
4. Anita Shapira, "The Eichmann Trial: Changing Perspectives," *Journal of Israeli History* 23, no. 1 (2004): 18–39.
5. Alexander Laban Hinton, "Afterword: Wonder Woman, the Gutter, and Critical Genocide Studies," in *Memory and Genocide: On What Remains and the Possibility of Representation*, Edited by Fazil Moradi, Ralph Buchenhorst and Maria Six-Hohenbalken (New York: Routledge, 2017), 168. For a helpful example of how Hinton operationalizes the ways that he views "critical genocide studies" see Alexander Labon Hinton, *Man or Monster: The Trial of a Khmer Rouge Torturer* (Durham: Duke University Press, 2016).
6. Hamza Karčić, "Remembering by Resolution: The Case of Srebrenica," *Journal of Genocide Research* 17, no. 2 (May 2015): 205–210.
7. See Alan J. Kuperman, "Humanitarian Hazard," *Harvard International Review* 26, no. 1 (Spring 2004): 64–68.
8. Critical genocide scholars could point out that various cultures and communities, before the popularization of Raphaël Lemkin's term "genocide," had used various rhetorical labels to describe the perpetration of wide-scale massacres of entire populations. For example, terms such as Norwegian *folkemord*, German *Völkermord*, the Greek *genoktonia*, and the Armenian

tseghaspanutiun were all used at different points in time to describe acts that some today call genocides. Matthias Bjornlund, "Integrating Genocide History," *Genocide Studies International* 12, no. 1 (Spring 2018): 129–146, 129.

9. Salman Rushdie et al., "The Rohingya Are Facing Genocide. We Cannot Be Bystanders," *The Guardian*, last modified November 10, 2017, https://www.theguardian.com/commentisfree/2017/nov/10/rohingya-genocide-ethnic-cleansing-never-again; Simon Adams, "Ratko Mladić, International Justice and the Bones of the Rohingya," *Huffington Post*, last modified November 24, 2017. http://www.globalr2p.org/media/files/ratko-mladic-international-justice-and-the-bones-of-the-rohingya-huffpost.pdf
10. George Steinmetz, "The First Genocide of the 20th Century and Its Postcolonial Afterlives: Germany and the Namibian Ovaherero," *The Journal of the International Institute* 21, no. 2 (Winter 2005): 1–8, https://quod.lib.umich.edu/j/jii/4750978.0012.201?view=text;rgn=main
11. Some interesting cases might have *both* "colonial" and "modern" features of genocides. See, for example, Yaroslav Bikinsky, "Was the Ukrainian Famine of 1932–1933 Genocide?" *Journal of Genocide Research* [illegible], no 2 (1999): 147–156.
12. *BBC News* Staff, "Mexico Demands Apology from Spain and the Vatican over Conquest," *BBC News*, last modified March 26, 2019, https://www.bbc.com/news/world-latin-america-47701876
13. Andrés Manuel López Obrador, quoted in *BBC News* Staff, "Mexico Demand Apology," paragraph 9.
14. *BBC News* Staff, "Mexico Demand Apology," paragraph 15.
15. Diego Torres, "Spain and Mexico's Centuries-Old Blame Game," *Politico*, last modified March 29, 2019, paragraph 22, https://www.politico.eu/article/spain-and-mexico-centuries-old-blame-game-diplomatic-spat-history-hernan-cortes/
16. Rafa Hernando quoted in Torres, "Spain and Mexico's," paragraph 22.
17. Josep Borrell, quoted in Torres, "Spain and Mexico's," paragraph 7.
18. For an intriguing discussion of some of the temporal and political features of many apologies for some contemporary collective memories of colonial wrongs see Matt James and Jordan Stanger-Ross, "Impermanent Apologies: On the Dynamics of Timing and Public Knowledges in Political Apology," *Human Rights Review* 19 (2018): 289–311.
19. For an example of an exception to this narrowness that moves in the direction that I am defending in this book see John Docker, "Raphaël Lemkin's History of Genocide and Colonialism," *United State Holocaust Memorial Museum*, February 26, 2004, https://www.ushmm.org/m/pdfs/20040316-docker-lemkin.pdf. See also Damien Short, *Redefining*

Genocide: Settler Colonialism, Social Death and Ecocide (New York: Zed Books, 2016); Bart Luttikhuis and A. Dirk Moses, *Colonial Counterinsurgency and Mass Violence: The Dutch Empire in Indonesia* (Milton Park, Abingdon: Routledge, 2014).

20. Some uses of the Greek mythological figure Pandora appear in discussions of the repatriation of indigenous artefacts. William S. Logan, "Closing Pandora's Box: Human Rights Conundrums in Cultural Heritage Protection," in *Cultural Heritage and Human Rights*, edited by Helaine Silverman and D. Fairchild Ruggles (New York: Springer, 2007), 33–52.
21. For more on these genocidal structures see Patrick Wolfe, "Settler Colonialism and the Elimination of the Native," *Journal of Genocide Research* 8, no. 4 (December 2006): 387–409; Donald Bloxham, "Organized Mass Murder: Structure, Participation and Motivation in Comparative Perspective," *Holocaust and Genocide Studies* 22, no. 2 (Fall 2008): 203–245.
22. Vahakn N. Dadrian, *The History of the Armenian Genocide: Ethnic Conflict from the Balkans to Anatolia to the Caucasus* (New York: Berghahn Books, 2004).
23. Mark Biondich, *The Balkans, Revolution, War and Political Violence since 1878* (New York: Oxford University Press, 2011); Hannibal Travis, "Constructing the 'Armenian Genocide': How Scholars Unremember the Assyrian and Greek Genocides in the Ottoman Empire," in *Hidden Genocides: Power, Knowledge, Memory*, edited by Alexander Laban Hinton, Thomas La Pointe and Douglas Irvin Erickson (New Brunswick: Rutgers University Press, 2013), 170–192.
24. For one of the key works that invited readers to broaden the circumference of guilt and drastically increase the numbers involved in carrying out Nazi genocidal schemes see Daniel Goldhagen, *Hitler's Willing Executioners* (New York: Alfred A. Knopf, 1996).
25. Timothy Snyder, *Bloodlands: Europe Between Hitler and Stalin* (New York: Basic Books, 2010).
26. For a fascinating round-table debate among academics about whether or not the Holocaust should be viewed as some type of a "colonial genocide," see Robert Pergher et al., "The Holocaust: A Colonial Genocide?" *Dapim: Studies on the Holocaust* 27, no. 2 (2013): 40–73. See also Donald Bloxham, *The Final Solution: A Genocide* (Oxford: Oxford University Press, 2009); Carroll P. Kakel, III, *The Holocaust as Colonial Genocide: Hitler's "Indian Wars" in the "Wild East"* (New York: Palgrave Pivot, 2013).
27. Janet Jacobs, *Memorializing the Holocaust: Gender, Genocide and Collective Memory* (London: I.B. Tauris, 2010).
28. We need to remember that some oppressed communities perpetuate their own genocides. See Nicholas A. Robins and Adam Jones, editors, *Genocide*

by the Oppressed: Subaltern Genocide in Theory and Practice (Bloomington: Indiana University Press, 2009).

29. Ljiljana Radonić. "From 'Double Genocide' to 'the New Jews': Holocaust, Genocide and Mass Violence in Post-Communist Memorial Museums," *Journal of Genocide Research* 20, no. 4 (November 2018): 510–52■.
30. Raz Segal, "The Modern State, the Question of Genocide, and Holocaust Scholarship," *Journal of Genocide Research* 20, no. 1 (January 2018): 108–133.
31. Nice summaries of some of the intentionalist-functionalist perspectival ways of reviewing the Holocaust are presented in Nigel Pleasants, "Ordinary Men: Genocide, Determinism, Agency, and Moral Culpability," *Philosophy of the Social Sciences* 48, no. 1 (2018): 3–32.
32. Christopher Powell, "What do Genocides Kill: A Relational Conception of Genocide," *Journal of Genocide Studies* 9, no. 4 (November 2007): 527–547.
33. Elisa Novic, *The Concept of Cultural Genocide: An International Law Perspective* (Oxford: Oxford University Press, 2016).
34. See Ann Curthoys, "Raphaël Lemkin's "Tasmania": An Introduction," *Patterns of Prejudice* 39, no. 2 (2005): 162–169.
35. Anti-imperialists were some of the critics of empire who complained about the perpetration of genocidal acts. See Philip Spencer, "Imperialism, Anti-Imperialism and the Problem of Genocide, Past and Present," *History* 98, no. 332 (October 2013): 606–622.
36. For key facets of these debates about Raphaël Lemkin's discussions of "biological" and "physical" destruction and the UN Convention on Genocide, see Michael A. McDonnell and A. Dirk Moses, "Raphaël Lemkin As Historian of Genocide in the Americas," *Journal of Genocide Research* 7, no. 4 (December 2005): 501–529.
37. See Raphaël Lemkin, "Genocide," *America Scholar* 15, no. 2 (April 1946): 227–230.
38. When Güenter Lewy wrote an essay for the *Journal of Genocide Research* that posed the question: "Can There be Genocide Without Intent to Commit Genocide?" this triggered a series of responses by interdisciplinary experts in the areas of genocide studies. See, for example, Tony Barta, "With Intent to Deny: On Colonial Intentions and Genocidal Denial," *Journal of Genocide Research* 10, no. 1 (March 2008): 111–119.
39. Norbert Finzsch, "If It Looks Like a Duck, If It Walks Like a Duck, if it Quacks Like a Duck," *Journal of Genocide Research* 10, no. 1 (March 2008): 119–126.
40. A. D. Moses, "Conceptual Blockages and Definitional Dilemmas in the "Racial Century": Genocides of Indigenous Peoples and the Holocaust." *Patterns of Prejudice* 36, no. 4 (2002): 7–36.

41. Ibid.
42. For a transnational way of viewing genocides in Europe that includes a critique of Auschwitz-centered analyses see Timothy Snyder, "In Defense of *Bloodlands*," *Tablet*, last modified August 3, 2012, https://www.tabletmag.com/jewish-arts-and-culture/books/108229/in-defense-of-bloodlands
43. For a recent example of how Professor Moses is willing to expand the genocidal categories see A. Dirk Moses, "'White Genocide' and the Ethics of Public Analysis," *Journal of Genocide Research*, March 29, 2019, https://www.tandfonline.com/doi/full/10.1080/14623528.2019.1599493
44. See Beth Van Schaack, "The Crime of Political Genocide: Repairing the Genocide Convention's Blind Spot," *The Yale Law Journal* 106, no. 7 (1997): 2259–2291.
45. The "Assyrian genocide" and the annihilation of the San in South Africa are just some of the many colonial genocides that need further investigation. See David Gaunt, "The Complexity of the Assyrian Genocide," *Genocide Studies International* 9, no. 1 (Spring 2015): 83–105; Mohamed Adhikari, *The Anatomy of South African Genocide: The Extermination of the Cape San Peoples* (Claremont: University of Cape Town Press, 2010).
46. For an example of a trenchant critique that explains how archival materials are used in "imaginary" ways to rhetorical configure beneficent settlers and colonial soldiers see Tilman Dedering, "The German-Herero War of 1904: Revisionism of Genocide or Imaginary Historiography?" *Journal of Southern African Studies* 19, no. 1 (1993): 80–88.
47. Totalitarian states are not the only organizations that carryout large-scale administrative massacres. Michael Mann, *The Dark Side of Democracy: Explaining Ethnic Cleansing* (Cambridge University Press, 2005).
48. Benjamin Meiches, *Genocide: A Political Genealogy* (Dissertation: Baltimore, MD: John Hopkins University, 2015).
49. For examples of twenty-first-century debates about statues, museums, and other memorializing devices see Ellie Hamrick and Haley Duschinski, "Enduring Injustice: Memory Politics and Namibia's Reparations Movement," *Memory Studies* 11, no. 4 (2018): 437–454; Simone Gigliotti, editor, *The Memorialization of Genocide* (New York: Routledge, 2016).
50. Saree Makdisi, "Elimination As a Structure: Tracing and Racing Zionism with Patrick Wolfe," *American Quarterly* 69, no. 2 (June 2017): 277–284.
51. Marouf Hasian, Jr., "The Diseased 'Terror Tunnels' in Gaza: Israeli Surveillance and the Autoimmunization of an Illiberal Democracy," *Media Tropes eJournal* 6, no. 2 (2016): 90–125.

52. As Raymond Evans explains, the term "indigenocide" is meant to be a term that references situations where observers may witness the perpetration of genocide, the destruction of human populations, ecocide, the destruction and theft of environments, and ethnocide, or the destruction of cultures. John Passant, "How the Rise of Trump is Related to Indigenocide and Australia Day," *Independent Australia*, last modified January 25, 2017, https://independentaustralia.net/australia/australia-display/how-the-rise-of-trump-is-related-to-indigenocide-and-australia-day,9962.
53. In the case of the Nabka debates see Zev Farber, "Palestinian Nakba and Israeli Independence: Telling Two Incomplete Stories," *The Times of Israel*, last modified May 15, 2018, https://blogs.timesofisrael.com/palestinian-nakba-and-israeli-independence-telling-two-incomplete-stories/
54. Sadly, the entrenched nature of some of these myths about "disappearing" or "vanishing" indigenous communities creates incredibly difficult political and social difficulties for the survivors and their descendants. See William R. Price, "Overcoming the Myth of Extinction: The Path Toward Heritage Rights for the Tasmanian Aboriginals," *Heritage & Society* 10 no. 1 (2017): 68–90.
55. Ibid., 69–70.
56. For an overview of some of this revisionism see Benjamin Madley, "From Terror to Genocide: Britain's Tasmanian Penal Colony and Australia's History Wars," *Journal of British Studies* 47, no. 1 (January 2008): 77–106.
57. Noam Sheizaf, "Despite Efforts to Erase It, the Nakba's Memory is More Present than Ever in Israel," *+972*, last modified May 14, 2013, https://972mag.com/despite-efforts-to-erase-it-the-nakbas-memory-is-more-present-than-ever-in-israel/71468/
58. For some fine introductory overviews that show how critical scholars might use deconstructive, Foucauldian, and other critical approaches in the study of genocides see Alexander Laban Hinton, "Critical Genocide Studies," *Genocide Studies and Prevention: An International Journal* 7, no. 1 (2012): 1–13, https://www.sciencespo.fr/mass-violence-war-massacre-resistance/en/document/toward-theory-critical-genocide-studies https://scholarcommons.usf.edu/cgi/viewcontent.cgi?article=1044&context=gsp; A. Dirk Moses, "Toward A Theory of Critical Genocide Studies," *Sciences Po*, April 18, 2008; https://www.sciencespo.fr/mass-violence-war-massacre-resistance/en/document/toward-theory-critical-genocide-studies; Andrew Woolford, *The Benevolent Experiment: Indigenous Boarding Schools, Genocide, and Redress in Canada and the United States* (Lincoln: University Of Nebraska Press, 2015).
59. Note, for instance, *History News Network* Staff, "Historian Taner Akçan's New Book Includes 'Smoking Gun' of Armenian Genocide," *History News Network*, last modified January 17, 2018, https://historynewsnetwork.

org/article/168025. For a trenchant critique of these "smoking gun" approaches see Raymond Evans, "Chapter 5: 'Crime Without a Name': Colonialism and the Case for 'Indigenocide,'" in *Empire, Colony, Genocide: Conquest, Occupation, and Subaltern Resistance in World History*, edited by A. Dirk Moses (New York: Berghahn Books, 2008), 133–147.

60. Damien Short, "When Sorry Isn't Good Enough: Official Remembrance and Reconciliation in Australia," *Memory Studies* 5 no. 3 (2012): 293–304.
61. James Daschuk, "When Canada Used Hunger to Clear the West," *The Globe and Mail*, last modified July 19, 2013, https://www.theglobeandmail.com/opinion/when-canada-used-hunger-to-clear-the-west/article13316877/
62. See Ann Laura Stoler, *Imperial Debris: On Ruins and Ruination* (Durham: Duke University Press, 2013).
63. Edward Said, *Orientalism* (New York: Vintage Books, 1979).
64. Judith Butler, *Parting Ways: Jewishness and the Critique of Zionism* (New York: Columbia University Press, 2012).
65. For an excellent explanation of Foucault's notion of *dispositif* as a massive governmental apparatus see Giorgio Agamben, *What is an Apparatus? And Other Essays* (Redwood City, CA: Stanford University Press, 2009).
66. For a popular illustration of how postcolonial scholars and other critical researchers can extend some of Foucault's work see Robert J. C. Young, "Foucault on Race and Colonialism," *New Formations* 25 (Summer 1995): 57–65; Pal Ahluwalia, "Post-Structuralism's Colonial Roots: Michel Foucault," *Social Identities* 16, no. 2 (2010): 597–606.
67. Michael Foucault, *Power/Knowledge: Selected Interview and Other Writings 1972–1977*, edited by Colin Gordon, translated by Colin Gordon, Leo Marshal, John Mepham and Kate Soper (New York: Pantheon, 1980), 93.
68. See Michael Mahon, *Foucault's Nietzschean Genealogy: Truth, Power, and the Subject* (Albany: SUNY Press, 1982).
69. Michel Foucault, "The Discourse on Language," in *The Archaeology of Knowledge* (New York: Pantheon, 1972), 215–237, 231–232.
70. Michel Foucault, *Knowledge, Discipline and Punish: The Birth of the Prison*, translated by Alan Sheridan (New York: Vintage, 1995).
71. Young, "Foucault on Race," 57–67.
72. Andrew Woolford and James Gacek, "Genocidal Carcerality and Indian Residential Schools in Canada," *Punishment & Society* 18, no. 4 (2016): 500–419, 401.
73. Ibid.
74. Stephen Winter, *Transition Justice in Established Democracy: A Political Theory* (Hampshire: Palgrave Macmillan, 2014), 217.

75. Benjamin Madley, *An American Genocide: The United States and the California Indiana Catastrophe, 1846–1873* (New Haven: Yale University Press, 2016).
76. For an excellent example of a comparative study of transcontinental ways of conceptualizing race, genocide, and assimilation, see Patrick Wolfe, "Land, Labor, and Difference: Elementary Structures of Race," *The American Historical Review* 106, no. 3 (June 2001): 866–905. I am indebted to Professor Wolfe for his delineation of confrontational, segregationist, conciliatory, and annihilationist settler colonial rhetorics.
77. Lorenzo Veracini, "Decolonizing Settler Colonialism: 'Kill the Settler in Him and Save the Man,'" *American Indian Culture and Research Journal* 41, no. 1 (2017): 1–18, 2.
78. Hannah Wylie, "Toward a Genealogy of Reconciliation in Canada," *Journal of Canadian Studies* 51, no. 3 (Fall, 2017): 601–635, 603.
79. Pamela Palmater, "Genocide, Indian Policy, and Legislated Elimination of Indians in Canada," *Aboriginal Policy Studies* 3, no. 2 (2014): 27–54, 32.
80. See, for example, Steven Katz, *The Holocaust in Historical Context. Volume I: The Holocaust and Mass Death Before the Modern Age* (Oxford: Oxford University Press, 1994. As Malcolm Bull points out in his review of the Katz' book in the *London Review of Books*:

> Steven Katz has set out to secure the boundaries of one contested area by proving that the Jews killed by the Nazis are the sole rightful inhabitants of the territory defined by the concept 'victims of genocide': 'The Holocaust is phenomenologically unique by virtue of the fact that never before has a state set out, as a matter of intentional principle and actualised policy, to annihilate every man, woman and child belonging to a specific people.' In the first of the projected three volumes this thesis is defined with ponderous rigour, and then defended in a historical survey of the pre-modern world that clings tenaciously but precariously to the mountainous footnotes beneath it. Subsequent volumes will cover the modern period, and the Nazi era itself. The object is to examine every putative instance of genocide before the Holocaust and demonstrate that it fails to fit the definition.

Malcolm Bull, "One and Only," *London Review of Books*, last modified February 23, 1995, paragraph 2, https://www.lrb.co.uk/v17/n04/malcolm-bull/one-and-only

81. Derek Gregory, *The Colonial Present: Afghanistan, Palestine, Iraq* (New York: Wiley-Blackwell, 2004).
82. Woolford and Gacek, "Genocidal Carcerality," 500–419.

CHAPTER 2

Remembering and Forgetting the Tasmanian Genocide

Abstract In this particular chapter the author defends the need for more debates about colonial genocides by focusing attention on the types of arguments that are advanced by scholars and activists who argue about the colonial-settler perpetration of a "Tasmanian genocide." While some skeptics of this thesis use Raphael Lemkin's definition of genocide to argue that only a few hundred Tasmanians died in conflicts like the Black War, there are others who are adamant that it is not the exact numbers who die that determines whether certain colonial acts constitute a genocide. The chapter puts on display evidence from public and academic sources to show that further debate is needed about the attempted "extirpation" of the Tasmanians.

Keywords Conciliation extirpation • Raphael Lemkin • Tasmania • The Black War

There is no question that an increasing number of academics—in both Tasmania and around the world—have been intrigued by the possibility that what some call the "Tasmanian genocide" might soon be included in more synthesized collections of studies of colonial or modern genocides.[1] Scholars today contend that between 1804 and 1856 thousands of indigenous Tasmanians lost their lives during conflicts with convicts, soldiers, and other settlers. At places like Risdon Cove near Hobart indigenous

M. Hasian, Jr., *Debates on Colonial Genocide in the 21st Century*,
https://doi.org/10.1007/978-3-030-21278-0_2

survivors during the twenty-first century participate in performative acts of remembrance to commemorate the Moomairremener Aboriginal people who died at Risdon Cove. Our descendants remember those who later dared the cross the "Black Lines" that were organized by settlers who talked about both "reconciliation" and "annihilation."[2]

Indigenous communities living on Tasmania have survived and flourished, and the 1995 return of a tiny portion of their land has not put an end to various requests for genocidal acknowledgments, apologies, or other forms of restorative justice.

New layers of arguments are added when disputes about the carrying out of colonial settler wars or massacres or genocides are tethered to rhetorical frames that are crafted by those who assume that few remember these sordid affairs. Some historians, like Nick Brodie, have written books, like *The Vandemonian War* (2016),[3] that have been marketing in ways that tantalize readers with promises of revelations about some "secret history" of British invasions and conquests. Benjamin Madley, writing in 2018, could note that "many have written about the state's role in the [Vandemonian] annihilationist war against Aboriginal Tasmanians."[4]

Yet there are also some researchers, like Güenter Lewy, who can find ways of arguing that imperial conflicts or colonial wars or internecine campaigns do not fit Raphael Lemkin's legalistic definition and should therefore not be compared with the World War II Holocaust.[5] More relevant in the Tasmanian situation is Henry Reynold's stance that the legalistic term "genocide" should be used in restrictive ways that would not apply to the 1804–1832 settler violence in Tasmania.[6] As late as 2014 John Howard, the former Australian Prime Minister, could confidently tell his listeners that there was no genocide of any indigenous Australians.[7]

What happened in Tasmania between 1804 and 1832 or between 1804 and 1872 continues to be contested historical terrain, and many continue to resist the idea that British colonizers, convicts, or other settlers intentionally carried out any "extirpation" of the Tasmanians. For example, skeptics of this genocidal thesis might note that some of the major conflicts that occurred between 1824 and 1831 may have cost the lives of over 1000 Tasmanians and settlers, but because the "Black War" did not involve the Australian Army it is not official recognized by the Australian Government as a war, much less some state-sponsored genocide.[8]

Kristyn Harman, a senior lecturer in history at the University of Tasmania, explained some of the potential reasons for this skepticism in 2018:

> Voluminous written and archaeological records and oral histories provide irrefutable proof that colonial wars were fought on Australian soil between British colonists and Aboriginal people. More controversially, surviving evidence indicates the British enacted genocidal policies and practices – the intentional destruction of a people and their culture.... Curiously, books published before and since [James] Bonwick's [1870] have stuck to a master narrative crafted during and immediately after the Tasmanian conflict. This held that the implementation and subsequent failure of conciliatory policies were the ultimate cause of the destruction of the majority of Tasmanian Aboriginal people. The effect of this narrative was to play down the culpability of the government and senior colonists.[9]

For a plethora of scholarly, political, and legal reasons, this master colonial settler narrative, which focuses on unsuccessful conciliatory efforts, continues to be used in ways that undermine the consciousness-raising efforts of Tasmanian activists and scholars who request that national and international communities write and talk about the lingering effects of a Tasmanian genocide. Penelope Edmonds has recent noted that the "question of whether reconciliation is possible, and if so, how" is not easy to answer in "the face of extreme frontier violence and genocide on the one hand, and a mythic nineteenth century 'Great Conciliation' of Aboriginal peoples and an erroneous 'extinction' narrative on the other."[10]

In this particular chapter I extend the work of critical genealogists, critical genocide scholars, colonial settler researchers, and others who are concerned about the pushback that has come when scholars have chipped away at the *mythos* that swirls around that benevolent, conciliatory tale that has been told about primarily peaceful settlement of Tasmania. I argue that only by admitting that we need more debate about these issues—and not pretending that archival matters are "settled"—can we decolonize that master narrative that Professor Harman referenced.

In many ways the twenty-first-century participants in conversations about whether we should acknowledge the existence of a Tasmanian genocide are oftentimes recirculating permutations of much older colonial and imperial arguments. Since at least the late 1830s a host of local, regional, national, and transatlantic communities have participated in heated debates about whether the early British convicts, settlers, missionaries, or colonial administrators who occupied "Van Diemen's Land" (the early name for Tasmania) should be blamed for the "extirpation" of the Tasmanian Aborigines.[11] "It is a paradox of world history," claims Anne Curthoys, that “while Tasmania, one of Australia’s six states and an island to the south of the Australian mainland, has long and frequently” been “cited internationally as having witnessed a clear-cut case of genocide, such a characterization is rarely adopted within Australia.”[12]

Some Australians would rather think of the positive sides of settler colonialism and the mythic farming of “unoccupied land” (*terra nullius*), but there are researchers and activists who are adamant that those involved in today’s reconciliation and multicultural efforts do not forget about some of the darker chapters of Australian histories. In 2016 Penelope Edmonds provided a fairly typical summary of some of this hauntology when she wrote:

> The Black War resulted in the almost wholesale slaughter of Aboriginal peoples on the island in a settler land war that many have argued was indeed genocidal. At the time of contact in 1803, it was estimated that around 6,000–8,000 people lived in Trowunna (the Aboriginal name for Tasmania), but that number was rapidly reduced to a remnant population. By 1838 only around 60 people had survived, many to be exiled against their will to northerly Flinders Island in the Bass Strait.[13]

Descendants of the European settlers who occupied Trowunna could characterize this as the unfortunate, but typical, loss of indigenous life that gets chronicled when violent communities have difficulties accepting segregationist, assimilationist, or conciliatory policies.

This all provides readers with an illustrative example of how some traditional or critical work gets marginalized for threatening foundational nationalist myths about frontier settlement heroism or beneficent British imperialism. One writer for *The Sydney Morning Herald* would write in 2002 that while “the brutal dislocation of Australia’s indigenous population has rightly become an acknowledged chapter of national shame, the accusation of genocide” is something else altogether.[14]

It will be my contention that critical genocidal critics can teach us a great deal about both the “extirpation” of the Tasmanian Aborigines and twenty-first-century appropriations of Tasmanian histories and public memories. Regardless of whether we view ourselves as social scientists who are trying to “set the record straight,” or humanists who are interested in the cultural contours of these debates, we have much to learn about the power/knowledge/discourse dimensions of the earlier nineteenth-century rhetorics that were produced by those who were trying to protect, or annihilate, the "Aborigines." It behooves as to see how presentist disputation about everything from land rights to the 2017 Tasmanian government's amendment of the old Relics Act of 1975 have been influenced by settler colonial mythologies. As late as 2017 William Price, after surveying how Tasmanians were debating about heritage legislation, was forced to conclude that it seemed as though many were oblivious to the fact that the "Tasmanian Aboriginals were the recipients of among the worst treatment of any Indigenous peoples in the colonial history of the British Empire."[15]

What accounts for the hesitancy of so many to at least acknowledge this particular genocide? Is it worries about potential costs of reparations that have influenced the German and Namibian reception of indigenous genocidal claims for what happened in "German South West Africa"? Is it because there is still disputation about the facticity of what happened during the "Black War" years? Are non-indigenous communities in Tasmania worried that they will be asked to give back more lands to Aboriginal communities? Or can this be viewed as yet another example of where national identify formation has everything to do with the reluctance to publicly debate about difficult heritages?

It is also fascinating to note how few are willing to note that Raphael Lemkin—who coined and helped popularize the term "genocide" during and after World War II—spent an inordinate amount of time in libraries studying archival materials on the "Black War" and other frontier conflicts in Tasmania. Orthodox Holocaust scholars and genocide researchers, who rarely reference Lemkin's work on Tasmania, may want to police the genocidal canons and keep this particular genocide out of anthologies because it involves colonial warfare and not "modern" administrative mass massacres.

Raphael Lemkin, along with Hannah Arendt and some of their other contemporaries,[16] recognized the need to understand some of the particular imperialist features of colonial genocides. However, before readers think that Lemkin was providing some totalizing decolonizing critique of British colonization we need to remember that he also argued that if the "Government devised some plan at the time of colonization for establishing the aborigines in one part of Tasmania and protecting them the attacks of the whites, the race might have been spared."[17]

Lemkin's generation appeared to believe that segregation and paternal protection of Aboriginal communities in Tasmania provided alternatives to annihilationist settler colonial practices. This legalistic fragment appeared to be taken from those older conciliatory constellations of meaning that were circulating for almost a century before the perpetration of the Holocaust.

Those who use Lemkin's commentaries on cultural genocide or the Tasmanian genocide to help with their critiques of settler colonial policies will find that they will soon be confronted with many ironies, contradictions, contingencies, and indeterminate ways of reading the Australian settler or indigenous archives. For example, Lemkin may not have realized that those in Hobart and colonial officials in London were oftentimes promoting those types of segregationist policies at the same time that they sanctioned the use of violent responses to "black" raids on farms or settlements. Some of the suggestions that he was offering looked very much like the "conciliatory" rhetorics that were circulated in the early 1830s.

While some scholars try to use Lemkin's work in their critiques of convict abuses in colonial Van Diemen's Land they sometimes fail to see how local settler discourses and British imperial rhetorics were a part of a much larger "visual, intellectual, and trans-imperial lexicon" that was formed by those who were concerned about "the cessation of violence, conciliation and Indigenous transformation."[18] In the name of "necessity" excessive violence could be rationalized as a way of saving the settlers from aborigines who would not "conciliate" and accept changing cultural and material relationships.

In the rest of this chapter I will provide readers with many different examples of how those who want to narrow our field of genocidal vision can focus on exclusionary interpretations of Lemkin's essays, or how skeptical reviewers of the Tasmanian genocide thesis can cite the formalistic work of UN drafters who wanted to highlight "biological" and "physical," but not "cultural" ways for defining genocides. In fascinating, and yet frustrating ways, Lemkin's name can be invoked by *both supporters and critics of the Tasmanian genocide thesis.*

I will also be illustrating in this chapter how various generations of scholars, investigative journalists, and others have quarreled about whether these Tasmanian topics are even debatable.

At this point in my critique I need to note that my Foucauldian, critical genealogical way of studying genocides focuses more on the contested ways that publics and decision-makers frame these issues than how a single individual like Lemkin wrote about genocides. I care a great deal about the rhetorical constraints that confront indigenous Tasmanian survivors who are asking for genocidal acknowledge, more equitable land redistribution, or apologies. When critical genocide scholars join the ranks of those who spend an inordinate amount of time dissecting Lemkin's archival works they intentionally or unintentionally help entrench the very legal frameworks that they try to decolonize elsewhere. I see no reason to adopt perspectival approaches that privilege legalistic frameworks that are produced and recirculated by those who want to focus their primary attention on the genocides that take place on the European continent. Nor do I have an interest in accepting the mythological idea that the Hobart or London attempts at "conciliation" provide evidence that officials who helped govern Van Diemen's Land had no interest in carrying out, or condoning, the "extirpation" of the indigenous Tasmanians.

I am also cognizant of the fact that some traditional Holocaust researchers or genocide scholars who extend Lemkin's work try to balance studies of agency with structural critiques, but far too often, when they adopt legalistic, Cold War ways of defining genocides they end up reproducing the very *epistemes* and structures that they think they are critiquing.[19] As Patrick Wolfe once noted, settler colonial arguments about land, labor, and cultural differences involved "elementary structures of race," that required the production of strategic confrontation, carceration, and assimilationist rhetorics.[20] Professor Wolfe defended the controversial position that oftentimes these were variants of annihilationist rhetorics.

Patrick Wolfe was convinced that while occasionally researchers might find examples of life-sparing efforts of colonizers—where Aboriginal women in Tasmania might be spared for sealing and oyster diving or Torres Strait Island men's lives were spared for labor—for the most part the "dominant pattern" that was manifest was the "decimation of the Aboriginal population."[21] Wolfe liked to compare and contrast the Australian carceral, segregationist, and assimilation strategies with the colonial settler structures of the USA and Brazil.

After reading the work of scholars like Wolfe I now take the position that those who study what scholars have to say about the Tasmanian genocide cannot avoid grappling *with the question of how audiences interpret and operationalize* Lemkin's work. They might admire his perseverance as he fought to have some of these ideas incorporated into the UN Convention and the Punishment of the Crime of Genocide that was presented in 1948 and finally adopted by many in 1951.[22] However, some audiences can admire Lemkin and still assiduously avoid writing about such topics as the loss of spirituality or community and the passage of laws prohibiting the carryout of "cultural" genocides.

I disagree with those scholars who try to "settle" some of this elite or public disputation by appealing to particular Archimedean, legalistic interpretations that have been crafted by individual judges, lawyers, law review writers, or commissioners. We need to listen to their voices, and we can include critiques of their work in any "decolonizing" efforts, but we should not privilege those elite voices as we study how indigenous and non-indigenous communities engage in dialogues about whether or not we need to recognize particular acts as genocidal in nature.

I therefore join those "critical" scholars who try to counter the hegemonic nature of some of this reliance on writers like Lemkin by critiquing not only "scholarly" work but the public texts and genealogies that are produced by investigative journalists, activists, and laypersons who become embroiled in heated disputation about colonial "wars," "atrocities," or genocides.[23]

Given my focus on public and legal disputation I cannot always be dismissive of the diverse Lemkin-like, legalistic frames that are used to discuss genocidal labeling, especially in cases where those jurisprudential frames are tethered to nationalistic and other rhetorical templates that are then used to deny, revise, or downplay the possibility that a Tasmanian genocide had been perpetrated by generations of settlers and their defenders.[24]

I would argue that from a critical genealogical vantage point—that tries to take into account the power/knowledge/discourse features of genocides and genocidal debates—the key here is keeping track of the *epistemes* and the other rhetorical units of analysis—what Foucault also called "elements"—that are produced by many collectives during a host of generational debates. Oftentimes, as I noted in the introduction to these chapters, this involves the critical review of indeterminate texts, illegible writings, and what Foucault called the "gray" that comes from studies of "entangled and confused parchments" in archives that have been "scratched over and recopied many times."[25]

This is especially the case when settler colonial referencing of terms such as "extirpation" or "atrocity" or "conciliation" become elements in the constitutive crafting of those confrontational, carceral, and assimilationist rhetorics that Patrick Wolfe referenced. Wolfe would contend that in spite of claims to the contrary, these terms were used to justify all sorts of annihiliationist policies in places like Tasmania.

Given the indeterminacy of all legal definitions and texts researchers and readers ought not treat Lemkin's claims or texts as some pristine, archival containers of received wisdom that can be used to end controversies in ways that usually favor the empowered defenders of the status quo. Empowered nations in the Global "North" are comfortable finding elitist ways to rationalize their dismissal of arguments on colonial atrocities that come from the Global "South." It could be argued that in Australia and Tasmania talk of being "sorry" is used to stave off other calls for reparations, repatriation, radical land redistribution, and other forms of restitution for colonial wrongs.[26] This quarantining of radical critique is one more manifestation of the lingering "truth effects" (Foucault) of those old confrontational, segregationist, conciliatory, and assimilationist rhetorics.

If twenty-first-century scholars and other readers are going to try and decode Lemkin's texts, then those who study the symbolic and material power of these interpretations need to contextualize the *practical applications of those texts* by studying not only the words and deeds of those were accused of carrying out the "extirpation" of the Tasmanians, but also the social agency of those who opposed them. For example, if we take a work like James Bonwick's *The Land of the Tasmanians* (1870),[27] we would find that the author of this work was cited by Raphael Lemkin, who then became convinced that Bonwick's work offered empirical evidence that at one time between 5000 and 7000 aborigines were living on "Van Diemen's Island." This is an example of those "recopied" archival materials that Foucault was writing about in 1971. Lemkin's extension of Bonwick's research seems to ignore, or marginalize, the positions of the Moomairremener Aboriginal communities or the other indigenous groups who wanted to refuse "conciliation" gestures that they sensed were being used to maintain power disparities.

Genealogical lines of argument that were circulating even before the time of Bonwick could then be bequeathed to Lemkin, who could link his own experiences of a divided Poland during World War II with the British colonization that began in 1804 and led "to the extermination of the Tasmanian aborigines in less than half a century."[28] This referencing of the extermination is laudable, but the mentioning of the absence of the constraining, protecting power of a benevolent state could be used to individuate colonial guilt. Lemkin, unlike critics like Patrick Wolfe, was unwilling to provide harsh critiques of all forms of predatory settler colonialism or European imperialism.

If critical genocide scholars actually followed Foucauldian admonitions that we concentrate on discursive formations instead of the agency of any single rhetor they would find that many of Lemkin's claims are themselves condensation symbols, fragmentary epistemic elements that had colonial origins. Lemkin was not only studying the colonial "context" that surrounded his neologism "genocide"—he was rhetorical (re)producing claims, evidence, and warrants that were produced by countless named and unnamed social agents who had been writing about "atrocities" and extirpation" for many, many generations.

Critical genocide scholars who adopt post-structural, Foucauldian, Derridean, and other "critical" approaches to Lemkin's words should not treat them as the gospel regarding what does, or does not, constitute a culpable genocide, but should instead view Lemkin's words as typical, World War II or Cold War shards of memory, foundational materials or debris from the past that are refashioned to suit the needs of present generations who argue over the Tasmanian genocide thesis.

These researchers who cared about these communal discursive formations would then try to be self-reflective about the potential motives of those who placed those materials in the archives in the first place. Those who adopted these perspectival ways of viewing arguments about genocides would refuse to treat any of these texts as arhetorical "primary" or "secondary" sources that provided disinterested historical information regarding "what happened" on Van Diemen's Island.

Lemkin's investigations of the "case" of the Tasmanian Aborigines, along with his readings of materials on the Armenian genocide and the destruction of Poland, helped convince Lemkin of the problematic nature of Allied World War II framings that highlighted military aggression but could not account for the specificity of genocidal acts like the Judeocide. All of the talk that he had to hear about the links between aggression and the rise of totalitarian states like Hitler's Nazi Germany, and all of the previous categorizations associated with "war crimes" failed to get at the essential characteristics of genocides.

The democratic nature of both British and Australian governance seems to have impacted the ways that various generations on several continents have debated about the Tasmanian genocide thesis. It is one thing to consider how genocides are carried out by totalitarian states, and quite another to factor in the atrocities that may have been committed by democratic states.

Even statistical information about the nature and scope of a colonial "massacre" becomes a source of contestation when we argue about potential genocidal acts that may have been committed by former colonial-settler states. Traditional scholars and critical researchers disagree about the specific causes of the Tasmanian "extirpation" and they also disagree about the numbers who may have died at places like Risdon Cove or the Three Thumbs forest or the areas near the infamous "Black Line."

The historians, demographers, and other researchers who are willing to call this a Tasmanian genocide usually contend that when British settlers arrived in Tasmania in 1803 there were probably somewhere between 4000 and 15,000 Aborigines living in that area, and that by 1835 there were fewer than 400 "full descent" Aboriginal Tasmanians left alive.[29] Critics of the Tasmanian genocidal "thesis" contend there is no way of substantiating these statistical claims.

In the same way that postcolonial writers can "deterritorialize" the work of Lemkin, critical genocide scholars can analyze and assess the selective public and elite readings that come from interpretative communities who argue about "the causes" of this decline. What is left in the archives, and what is considered relevant to this debate about Tasmanian "extirpation," often depends on one's subject position, one's sacred or secular beliefs, one's identification with a preferred means of analyzing texts, and one's feelings regarding the groups that are characterized as perpetrators, victims, or bystanders. Given the fact that the victors are the ones who usually get the dominant say in the collection of archival materials, this means that it is not unusual to find more "critical" voices calling for study of dominant *epistemes* as well as the "minority literatures" (Gilles Deleuze and Félix Guattari) that have been bequeathed to all of us.[30]

With this in mind, the rest of this chapter is organized in ways that help readers see both the diachronic and the synchronic dimensions of the confrontational, the carceral, the assimilationist, or the annihilationist rhetorics that circulated for decades in Australia. As Shayne Breen once explained, the "ways in which" rapid Aboriginal depopulation has been "portrayed by historians—extermination, extinction, dispossession and the more recently" discussion of "genocide" have "been matters of dispute since the 1980s and remain so to this very day."[31]

I will begin by providing a brief overview of some of the ideological features of dominant colonial settler texts, as well as "minority literatures" that were used to explain the alleged "demise" of indigenous Tasmanians. This is then followed by a second subsection that unpacks some of the discourses that were assembled between 1830 and 1867 as various colonial communities on the periphery, and in the metropole, tried to make sense of the deaths of so many Tasmanians. This is followed by a third portion of the chapter that explains why the discourse about "vanishing" Tasmanians itself seemed to disappear from view in most mainstream settings in Australia between 1875 and 1975. The fourth part of the chapter then takes up the topic of the resurrection of that "Tasmanian genocide thesis" during the late twentieth and early twenty-first centuries, and I explain how generational factors converged to catalyze the efforts of those who wanted to debate about the need to provide various forms of Aboriginal redress. The concluding section of the chapter then explains how renascent interest in the Tasmanians has impacted twenty-first-century debates about inclusive or exclusive ways of viewing genocides.

Contemplating the Ideological Nature of Texts: Documenting the Demise of the Tasmanians

Some scholars do not hesitate to name names as they comment on the culpability of the administrators, soldiers, settlers, and others who came up with a whole host of rationalizations for the removal of the indigenous Tasmanians who were living in this region before 1803.

Penelope Edmonds has explained how researchers have noted that on May 3, 1804, Lieutenant William Moore, the commanding officer of a British garrison at Risdon Cove, ordered troops to fire on Moomairremener Aboriginal people, who were "passing through on a kangaroo drive."[32]

Anna Johnston, who studied how "colonial celebrities" like George Augustus Robinson posed as "reconciliators," pointed out how some of the commentary about the decimation of these Aborigines appeared in scientific-looking frameworks that regarded some of these early contacts in this region as *colonial experiments* in colonized—colonizer relationships. She explains that "indigenous people" were "caught up in nineteenth-century imperial media cultures, sentimental racism, scientific racism and commodity racism."[33]

Some defenders of the Tasmanian genocide thesis focus on both the activities of single individuals as well as the larger structural or functional features of the colonial apparatus that was operating in this part of Australia. Benjamin Madley, for example, argued in 2008 that "Britain's Tasmanian colonial project, in combination with a culture of terror and official failure to protect Aborigines, opened the door to catastrophe."[34] Confrontational meetings led to raids that in turn led to arguments about the need to incarcerate, segregate, or conciliate the "Aborigines" who stood in the path of those who wanted to leave Hobart and colonize other parts of Van Diemen's Land.

These types of harsh critiques have produced scholarly work that points out that the British colonizers and the settlers coveted indigenous lands, and that the nineteenth-century writers who commented on "vanishing Aboriginal races" oftentimes supported the efforts of missionaries or British humanitarians who were trying to intervene in settler-aboriginal conflicts. A whole welter of devious and sinister motives went into the co-production of dense settler colonial *epistemes* regarding "natural" or necessitous frontier violence.[35]

That said, were the missionaries and the conciliators part of the solution, or were they a part of the problem? "In New South Wales and Tasmania, and to a lesser degree in Victoria and Queensland," argued Thomas James Rogers and Stephen Bain, researchers "have tended to blame convict-class rural workers for violence on the frontier."[36]

Did administrators', missionaries', or others' assimilationist or carceral rhetorics—that were often used to counter annihilationist tendencies—put on display that genocidal, Lemkin-like "intent" that I alluded to earlier in this chapter? Or were these examples of discourses that could be used by those who objected to the idea of having anyone witness any "cultural" or "physical" Tasmanian genocide?

Part of the heuristic value of critical genocide studies, or colonial genocidal studies, comes from the ways that these types of approaches invite readers and scholars to pay attention to the rhetorical cultures that infused these debates with symbolic and material meanings. It is fascinating to see the ways that twenty-first-century debates about Australian textbooks or historiography on the "dying" Tasmanian populations often recycle some of the very same arguments that appeared in nineteenth-century scientific tracts or newspaper articles regarding the causes of Tasmanian morbidity and mortality.

Even sympathetic members of Aboriginal Protection Societies, who felt that they were extending the work of earlier generations of anti-slavery advocates, may have had a difficult time seeing the structural or functional dimensions of this loss of life in places like Tasmania. Moreover, what was happening in Van Diemen's land was viewed by most colonial authorities in London as an experiment that would also help other parts of the British empire cope with their own aboriginal "natives" who either accepted, or rejected, European settler dispossession and domination. Relatively few critics of empire, before the end of the twentieth century, characterized this as a form of what would later be called indigenocide.[37]

Participants in these heated colonial or "Australian history" debates have at times adopted the position that we don't need to go through the dustbins of history and label each and every bloody colonial confrontation with indigenous communities as some type of genocidal encounter. Imagine how many times settlers and indigenous communities came into "contact" with one another and did not annihilate "the other," and critics of the "Tasmanian Genocide thesis," like John Dawson, would argue some revisionism amounted to "Van Demonisation."[38] Dawson opined that "Australian history" should not be treated as a "find-the-genocide game," and he was convinced that those who were playing this game found little evidence of mounting "exterminating" massacres, official planning, or complicity.[39] Dawson's book, *Washout*, warned readers about the "fabrication of Aboriginal history."[40]

Although many critical genocide scholars and colonial researchers refuse to accept Dawson's explanations, readers need to be cognizant of the suasory power of this type of neo-liberal position that reflects some of hermeneutics of suspicion that still swirls around talk of any Tasmanian genocide.[41] A popular position to take in these debates is that academics need to follow the lead of sensible politicians who are circumspect in the ways that they talk about the need for unilateral or multilateral interventionism in the name of stopping genocide. For example, before rushing to judgment, and before claiming that the Tasmanian Aborigines were the victims of genocide, doesn't it behoove twenty-first-century writers and audiences to think about the presence or absence of genocidal "intent" before they smear the good name of historical figures, places, or nation-states?

Other participants in these debates adopt more moderate neo-liberal stances on the "dying" Tasmanians, where arguers acknowledge that disease and violent conflicts led to the loss of many Aboriginal lives, but then they go on to argue that we need to contextual these as ***the unintended consequences*** of settler wars, accidents, or a "national tragedy."[42] For example, some Australian and British defenders of colonial or imperial policies have responded to these genocidal claims by alleging that today's discussions of political correctness, the need to respect indigenous rights, multiculturalism, the importance of postcolonial studies, or talk of national apologias has led to problematic revisionism. For those who adopt this stance, not all recorded histories of colonial massacres contain evidence of intentional annihilationist sentiments.

Again, readers in Tasmania, Australia, or elsewhere are provided with a permutation of Lemkin-type interpretations that can acknowledge that a few individual British settlers *might* have engaged in carrying out mass violence in Van Diemen's Land or in Tasmania, and yet they can avoid going the next step and calling this systematic indigenocide or genocide. They can cite some of the textual materials that came from a Lieutenant Governor of this colony, Sir George Arthur, who wrote in private correspondence in 1825 that he had to cope with a "vast deal of Crime amongst the Prisoners, murders, constant robberies, and other atrocious acts."[43] Arthur could be configured as a sage magistrate who tried to protect both settler and Aboriginal rights through segregationist or conciliatory practices.

Some writers refuse to accept this more moderate stance, and they adamantly refuse to acknowledge the possibility that more than a few settlers, colonial administrators, or London superiors invited or participated in the "extirpation" of the Tasmanians. Those who adopt these strict, intentionalist approaches often argue that all of this talk of Australian involvement in genocides is highly politicized, imaginative mythologizing that tells us more about the politics of the critics than it does about the actual "history" of Tasmania. Keith Windschuttle, for example, wrote several essays and books that attacked the notion that anyone in the Australian colonies had participated in any intentional or systematic genocide.[44] He would become the darlings of those who claimed that evidence-based historiographies were the key to refuting those obsessed with the "Tasmanian genocide hypothesis."

These contemporary contested histories and cultural memories—that are *all* politicized debates—can be linked to several earlier generational clusters of arguments that can be traced back to the late 1830s. This is the reason why some have written about how the Tasmanian Aborigines entered a prefigured, geopolitical world where imperial rhetorics "ensnared" locals and entangled them in the "metropolitan discourses far from their local environments."[45] For example, a nineteenth-century Oxford expert on "political economy," Herman Merivale, working 15,000 miles away from Tasmania, would assert that by 1842 the "Nation of Van Dieman's Land [was] reduced to a few families by long maltreatment." He explained that "settlers" shot "them down in the woods, or laid poisoned food within their reach."[46] Merivale felt that he was forced to conclude that the "history of European settlements" in Australia presented "a wide and sweeping destruction of native races by the uncontrolled violence of individuals and colonial authorities, followed by tardy attempts on the part of governments to repair the acknowledge crime."[47]

Merivale's early critiques—that represented the views of a minority of nineteenth-century observers—would provide some of the rhetorical elements and templates that would be picked up by many indigenous writers and "critical" genocide scholars when they made similar arguments more than 150 years later.

Merivale's critique provides an example of a "minor literature," a textual fragment that did not resonate with those who disagreed with this framing of Aboriginal absence and presence. Most British observers in the metropole seemed to treat the Tasmanians as the victims of convicts and settlers on the periphery, who were so far away from their homeland that they had forgotten what it meant to be "British." This type of nationalistic and imperial commentary reminds all of us of the importance of class prejudices that critical genocide scholars can use to augment analysis that highlight the racial features of these colonial rhetorics. Blaming the convicts and settlers for their lack of adherence to British imperial norms allowed the British to chastise the "degenerates" at the same time that they defended more enlightened frontier settlement. Defenders of the empire could use frames that highlighted the eugenically inferiority of the violent convicts at the same time that they defended Albion. Talk of the atrocious behavior of former Britons could be used to *individuate the acts* of those who were said to *have deviated* from imperial or colonial norms when they tried to annihilate the Tasmanian Aborigines. Official segregationist, carceral, and conciliatory policies were supposed to help those black aborigines who were slowly "dying" from identifiable or mysterious causes.

As readers might imagine, the settlers who populated Van Diemen's Land or the other colonies in Australia or New Zealand resented these arrogant dissociative tactics that were sometimes used by those who criticized excessive settler violence, and they in turn have left us journalistic shards of memory that represented their reactions to these critiques from places like London. Sometimes these settlers, and their descendants, rationalized the violence around them as *necessitous responses to barbarian attacks* on the colonial periphery that could not possibly be understood by those who were not facing Aboriginal spears. As Penelope Edmonds would note, throughout the "Australian colonies, calls for conciliation had come most often at times of severe violence: conciliation and capture would go hand in hand."[48] When the Aboriginal leader Umarrah was captured by some of Governor Arthur's subalterns Umarrah indicated that because his captors "had driven his people from their kangaroo hunting grounds" he had a duty to kill as many white people as possible.[49] Governor Arthur imprisoned Umarrah for a year and tried to persuade him that he needed to tell his people about the government's good intentions, but Umarrah escaped.

In theory, the tacit knowledge that was gained by former convicts, imperial administrators like Governor Arthur, and others who were living on the frontier was something that could not be understood by Parliamentarians or members Aboriginal Societies who did not witness the horrors of the "Black Wars."

Only by understanding some of these competitive, partial, contingent, and contradictory rhetorical histories of the supposed "extinction" of the Tasmanian Aborigines can scholars and other readers understand the volatile nature of the contemporary disputes that take place as national and international communities look back on these years and converse about colonial genocides, a Tasmanian genocide, or the inherently genocidal nature of all Australian frontier settlement.

Settling Van Diemen's Land and the Early Colonial Contextualizations of the "Extirpation" of the Tasmanian Aborigines, 1830–1873

During the late 1780s British explorers and settlers turned their attention to Van Diemen's Land, and since that time our archives have filled up with competing metanarratives that are deployed by those who try to explain why these Tasmanian "wars" killed thousands of Aborigines who died in Tasmania between 1803 and 1847.[50] Those who dispute some of these framings of colonial historical events, like Benjamin Madley, have reviewed journalistic commentaries, diary accounts, and other materials from this period so that they can critique the traditional work of scholars like Henry Reynolds.

Madley, like several other scholars who want to study colonial genocides, has been willing to defend the thesis that for "75 years after 1803 British policies led to the destruction" of thousands of indigenous Tasmanians, and he opined that most of this loss of life had taken place between 1803 and 1847. As far as Madley was concerned, conflicts between indigenous peoples and settlers over access to natural resources and control of territory did not always have to lead to wars or genocides, but when "economic competition becomes a zero-sum game" then violence escalates.[51] This suggested that critical scholars need to attend to those discursive records that might help pinpoint when certain opinions hardened and became annihiliationist, or when views were radicalized.[52]

Madley, unlike some of the conventional historians, wanted to underscore the point that when the white populations of Tasmania grew from over 5000 to more than 18,000 between 1820 and 1828[53] this meant that "British pastoral settlement" brought economic, political, and social tensions. Hundreds of thousands of sheep were brought to the island and the colonial government granted vast tracts of land to the settlers who were supposed to develop the land. The inference could be made that the handing over of indigenous lands to those involved in sheep herding was an example of state-sponsored activities that inevitably contributed to Aboriginal dispossession, and that it could be anticipated that this, in turn, would lead to horrific massacres.

Are readers willing to consider this type of incremental dispossession to be a sign of cultural genocide? Or is more proof required?

By 1822, out of the more than 12,000 whites who were living in Van Diemen's Land some 68 percent of them were convicts or former convicts.[54] Officials running Van Diemen's Land had to solve local problems that were allegedly caused by social agents who were banished from mainland Australian penal communities.[55] Journalists who wrote for the *Colonial Times* in 1826 were complaining about the inhumane and the torturous treatment of Aborigines or convicts.[56]

Places like Port Arthur—that became the port of entry for many convicts—was turned into an "Earthly hell"[57] and the all of the "trauma and violence that touched thousands" seemed to have "eroded cultural prohibitions against torturing children."[58] For critical scholars who followed the lead of Patrick Wolfe and saw settler violence as a "structure and not an event" (see the introduction),[59] affairs on Tasmania were spiraling out of control.

British observers expressed ambivalent feelings when they read or heard about convict abuses or settler-colonial retaliatory raids against the Aborigines. On the one hand, they wanted to encourage and support British imperial expansionism, but on the other hand, it needed to be done in ways that looked as though they were preserving Aboriginal lives.

The production of the self-serving framings of the early violence on Tasmania allowed both conservative British Tories and liberal Whigs to deflect attention away from the structural violence that came from colonial settlement as Britons highlighted the role that unruly "convicts" played during reconciliation efforts. In Bonwick's *Last of the Tasmanians* one ex-bushranger is quoted as saying that he would shoot down Aborigines in the same way that he shot "so many sparrows."[60]

Here it is the callousness of the former convicts, and not British or local governance, that is blamed for inciting trouble between peaceful settlers and local Aborigines. These colonial elements or *epistemes* provided the rhetorical fragments for those who would later be involved in future neo-liberal mythologizing.

Respectful Britons—the right type of settlers—were characterized in nineteenth-century pamphlets, books, and newspaper articles as the conciliatory parties who tried to stem the violence that came from the excesses of both the bushrangers and the barbarous Aborigines. For example, the *Hobart Town Gazette* and the *Colonial Times* contained articles that were written by those in the 1820s who lauded the efforts of various lieutenant governors and other officials. These were the colonial social agents who tried to use police actions, the recruitment of volunteers, bounties, and even public executions to control the threat of the bushrangers.[61] These were characterized as activities that maintained law and order.

Rather than viewing the convict system as an inherent part of exploitative frontier settlement schemes, the efforts of the colonial administrators were rhetorical framed as the necessitous acts of benevolent reformers who were aiding the cause of peaceful settlement by trying to prevent excessive local violence. Aborigines were supposed to understand that their survival, and their treatment, would depend on their acceptance of changing Social Darwinian realities.

Many of these hagiographic and patriotic accounts of the social agency of the administrators, police, and settlers in Van Diemen's Land used figurative templates that were used over and over again to remind readers of the coming "extermination" of both the bushrangers and the Tasmanian Aborigines. In 1827, for example, the *Colonial Times* would report that settlers who suffered from the raids of the Tasmanians, would "omit no step whereby" they might "destroy the black tribes even to utter extermination."[62] A frustrated Lieutenant Governor, in a letter to his superior in London, warned in 1830 that the "aboriginal race" would be "exterminated" because the Tasmanians could not accept being captured or "conciliated."[63] "Self-preservation," noted Lieutenant Governor Arthur, might "compel the inhabitants to destroy them."[64]

In spite of this race war type of rhetoric, few settlers were asked to put a stop to British colonization, frontier expansionism, or white settlement. The idea that Aboriginal Tasmanians had sovereign, and exclusive, land rights in Van Diemen's Land would have been laughable for many settlers, soldiers, and their supporters.

A perusal of the old Van Diemen's Land archival materials also served the cause of more moderate contemporary writers who wanted to talk about colonial "wars" and not genocides. More than few patriotic British or Australian scholars underscored the point that Britons accepted, and embraced their role as protectors of the indigenous groups. However, as Professor Plomley would claim in 1992, the difference often was that while European settlers who killed the Tasmanians could get away with murder under colonial law or the informal rules of settlement the "Aborigines could not."[65] Abstract theories about governmental protections for indigenous communities had to give ground when they came up against the practical rationalizations for hasty settler frontier expansionism.

While imperial reformers thousands of miles away worried about the preservation of the "British character" that was threatened by the "miscreants" who were robbing, murdering, and raping settlers or aborigines, local authorities in Australia or Van Diemen's Land produced their own genres that underscored the point that they did not have the luxury of trying to "conciliate" with local indigenous communities. Colonial administrators, the soldiers who were sent to protect settlers, and the defenders of the settlers' actions thought that idealistic British superiors knew little about the trials and tribulations of the settlers who suffered from "black" raids. By 1826, argues Professor Madley, some Aboriginal Tasmanians had resorted to "a desperate low-intensity guerilla war" that killed "isolated white settlers and convicts."[66] The settlers and convicts retaliated, and this brought spirals of epistemic and physical violence.

In his private correspondence Lieutenant Governor George Arthur mentioned that Tasmanian aboriginal leaders were complaining about how white people were taking possession of their land, destroying their natural food, the kangaroo, and were encroaching upon their sacred burial grounds,[67] but this empathic reading did not translate into any major calls for the cessation of frontier settlement.

Sadly, clusters of confrontational, segregationist, conciliatory, and annihilationist settler argumentative fragments can be folded into a larger colonial settler *dispositif* that rationalized the settler destruction of Aboriginal societies on Tasmania. Those who used their argumentative clusters agreed that the indigenous communities had to eventually submit to settler rule—they simply disagreed about the speed of land possession or the degree of violence that would be required for submission and deterritorialization.

In November of 1826 an obviously frustrated Lieutenant Governor Arthur—who had perhaps convinced himself that he had tried reconciliation first—issued an order that was recorded in the *Hobart Town Gazette* that explained to readers how, if "Native tribes" were determined to attack, rob, or murder "White inhabitants" then "any Persons" could arm themselves and join the military that would treat the native tribes as "open enemies."[68] Most interdisciplinary scholars who study the period between 1826 and 1833 seem to agree that it would be during these years that thousands of Tasmanians lost their lives.

The prefigurative confrontational, segregationist, conciliatory, and exterminationist genres that were produced during the second quarter of the nineteenth century provided the rhetorical materials that would later by redeployed by those who debated about whether all of this constituted a "war" (that theoretically does not deserve apologies or reparations) or a "genocide" that requires acknowledgment and other forms of restorative justice.

Oftentimes these debates about a colonial "war" or "massacre" or "genocide" revolve around issues of the agency of the Tasmanian Aborigines or the intents or actions of the colonial settlers. For example, Lyndall Ryan explained that governmental expropriation of land meant that the settlers were getting what the Aboriginal Tasmanians viewed as theirs, and they rose up and fought the invaders.[69] Ryan's work on the number of dead in the "Tasmanian War" would be discussed in the pages of *The Sydney Morning Herald*.[70]

In spite of the paucity of settler archival records[71] that can document the argumentative views of these Aborigines there is evidence that conciliators and other stakeholders in these disputes did not hesitate to write about the enslavement of indigenous communities, the rape of Aboriginal women, or the abduction of Aboriginal children.[72] George Augustus Robinson, whose famous journals are still considered by some to be authentic archival materials, wrote pages that were filled with recordings of abductions, instances of torture, and abuses by convicts and sealers. Genocide scholars and others have noted how Robinson used some of these texts to position himself as a peacekeeper who tried to help both the settlers and the Aborigines.[73]

Over time, as different nineteenth-century generations mulled over what to think about this early settler violence, new layers of dehumanizing, segregationist, or conciliatory rhetorics could be added to rationalize this mayhem. After the appearance of Charles Darwin's work those interested in applying the tenets of British racial science could treat the Aborigines as if they were on the lowest rung of social Darwinian ladders,[74] while settlers who wanted even more self-defense rationales could explain how indigenous tribes were threatening those who were traveling on island roads. Those who worried about being speared in the back by black Tasmanians did not discriminate between friend or foe. One settler, David Burn, would write in *Pictures of Van Diemen's Land* that the "aboriginal warfare was much more dreaded by the settlers than the attacks of the bushrangers."[75] In his *Extracts* Backhouse indicated that those around him considered the Aboriginal Tasmanians to be the "most degraded class of savages."[76]

One of the key issues for readers of this chapter, of course, is whether all of these argumentative recordings of frontier violence can be used for present-day, (post)colonial allegations of colonial genocide. If so, who should be held responsible for these horrific activities?

Although critics of Tony Barta or other critical genocide scholars like to claim that it was the 1990s cultural wars that helped usher in the new forms of revisionism that questioned the mainstream histories of Tasmania, a review of key archival materials reminds us that these types of questions occupied the attention of earlier generations who lived in Hobart, who resided on other parts of Van Diemen's Land, or who reviewed the sources of this violence from thousands of miles away. Henry Melville, a journalist who wrote *The History of the Island of Van Diemen's Land from the Year 1824 to 1835*, was convinced that settlers were responsible for the perpetration of abominable acts against aboriginal women:

> The stock-keepers may be considered as the destroyers of nearly the whole of the aborigines ... they thought little or nothing of destroying men for the sake of carrying to their huts the females of the tribe; and, if it were possible in a work like this to record but a tithe [one-tenth] of the murders committed on these poor harmless creatures, it would make the reader's blood boil cold at the bare recital.[77]

Melville seemed to have representing views of a few editors of local newspapers in places like Hobart who disagreed with the settlers and administrators who defended the harsh treatment of Aboriginals during the so-called race or extermination wars.[78]

These 1830s' remarks would be the types of rhetorical fragments that could be (re)assembled in dissenting or counter-colonial stories—those minor literatures or Foucauldian *epistemes*—that would interrogate some of justifications for settlement that would be produced by an assortment of British missionaries, local magistrates, journalists, even members of Aboriginal protection societies.

Melville did more than just serve for a number of years as the editor of the *Colonial Times*. He would also leave to posterity articles, lectures, and books on the Aboriginal "extirpation." In *The History of Van Diemen's Land* (1836) Melville recorded how there had been "few events" that had "tarnished the history of any colony more than in the manner in which the civilized portions of society conducted themselves towards" the indigenous communities.[79]

Ambiguous, but passionate talk about the prevention of violent conflict served the cause of those who wanted to legitimate frontier expansionism. John West, a Congregationalist minister, would write in his own history of Tasmania that locals on the island were "distinguished for the malicious vigour with which they traced and murdered the native people."[80]

Those who debate about the presence or absence of genocidal intent often get into heated disputation about the success or failure of the famous "Black Line," where some 2200 police, convicts, settlers, and others tried to clear the Aborigines out of the "settled districts" of the Island by herding them onto the southeasterly Tasmanian Peninsula.[81] Recorded remembrances of this event highlight the point that this particular 1830 project was undertaken during a period when there were less than 300 surviving Aborigines on the island, and those who participated in this ritual were ridiculed by those who pointed out that this was a farce. The line only captured two Tasmanians—an old man and a young boy, and on several occasions chiefs Mannalargenna, Umarrah, and Wareternatterlargener were able to lead small groups of Aborigines who breached the Black Line at places like Three Thumbs.[82]

Other settlers were convinced that the formation of the Black Line helped with segregationist efforts that encouraged the surviving Aborigines to stay away from the settled districts.[83] Shayne Breen contends that given the fact that these activities were intended to "secure widespread seizure of Aboriginal land," and that the Black Line helped with the forcibly removal of the Tasmanians from particular regions, the Black Line needs to be labeled as a "central instrument in the Tasmanian genocide."[84] This would be an example of Michel Foucault would characterize as a governmental apparatus. Critical genocide scholars or postcolonial critics might view this Black Line as exactly the type of colonial settler apparatus that appeared in the guise of segregationist reformation that nevertheless led to more and more violence and dispossession.

While some characterized the archival recordings of the infamous Black Line of 1830 as historical evidence that colonial settlers were willing participants in Governor's Arthur's genocidal schemes writers like Nicholas Clements used accounts from the settlers about the Black Line to illustrate how the Line was far from some organized state activity that united soldiers, settlers, and convicts. In his review of Clements' book Russell McGregor highlights the trials and tribulations of settlers and their protectors who were characterized as "cold and wet, ragged and often shoeless" holders of Black Line, who were also "poorly led, demoralized, and increasingly disillusioned by the whole enterprise."[85]

How, one might ask, could these ragged settlers and soldiers be acting in concert in ways that evidenced any collective genocidal intent, to wipe out the Aboriginals? Weren't they simply trying to incarcerate or segregate these indigenous communities?

The inference that might be reached by those who did not want to call this genocidal was clear—those whites who became part of the Black Line could hardly be viewed as perpetrators of mass atrocities. These soldiers and settlers who gathered together to form the Black Line were so disorganized and so worried that they hardly constituted any major threat to any indigenous population.

Colonial apologists and others might also want to point out that the lieutenant governors who promoted initiatives like the Black Line were assailed from all sides of these disputes by those who pressed the authorities for complementary or contradictory ways of handling the perceived Tasmanian "problem." In England, during the fall of 1834, abolitionists like Charles Buxton adopted the subject position of an Aboriginal defender who was willing to call on Parliament to protect, and to "Christianize" the "native" peoples within British imperial realms.[86] In places like London and Edinburgh arguments were circulated by missionaries who complained about the lack of religiosity on the part of the convicts and others on the colonial periphery, and this lack of religiosity was said to have contributing to the witnessing of the "Black Wars" in places like Tasmania.

Imperial administrators were thus pressured to put in place a temporary scheme called the "Protectorate." The Protectorate, argues Alex Tyrrell, was

> an example of the British parliament's willingness to safeguard the weak and powerless. Aboriginal Protectors were similar in some ways to the Special Magistrates who were appointed to supervise the transition from slavery in the West Indies after 1834 or to the inspectors who were appointed by legislation during the 1830s to enforce the regulations related to the employment of women and children in British factories.[87]

This type of philanthropic thinking—involving various gendered, class, and racialized roles—may have made complete sense to those who were 15,000 miles away from Hobart, but it must have seemed utopian to the settlers, sealers, and sheepherders who claimed that they were dodging spears in Tasmania.

A key historical figure in many of these British colonial social dramas was the protagonist, Governor George Arthur. One of the leading Australian historians of this period, Henry Reynolds, adopted a moderate stance when he claimed in 2004 that scholars could not answer with "any certainty" the question of whether "Governor Arthur strayed over the unmarked border" between warfare and "genocide."[88]

Again, these types of twenty-first-century conjectures were nothing new. By 1835, after several years of having to suffer through what amounted to open season on Aborigines following the passage of martial law edicts in Van Diemen's Land, it was said that only about 400 "full-descent" Aboriginal Tasmanians were left alive.[89] In the same ways that other imperialists tried to give the impression that they were looking out for their "native" wards British administrators during the mid-1830s placed surviving Tasmanians in offshore camps—in places like Flinders Island—to protect them from the settlers and the convicts.[90]

Yet in spite of these segregation efforts—that themselves were controversial—the Tasmanians were often configured by the 1860s as a "dying" race that came into contact with superior races. As Professor Breen explains, the death of "Truganini" during the 1870s was configured as the end of the Tasmanians. In the fanciful British accounts that circulated during this period the evolutionary fitness of the "pure, white-blooded English" could be contrasted with the "pre-ordained" passage of the uncivilized inferior races. The "pervasive acceptance of the extinction myth" Breen noted, was "reinforced by a monumental act of historical forgetting" as the colony changed its name from Van Diemen's Land to Tasmania.[91]

Strategic Forgetting, Nationalistic Amnesias, and Recontextualizations of the "Vanishing" Tasmanians, 1874–1975

The chronicled death of Truganini intrigued many British race scientists, civil servants, and historians of the era who were trying to make sense out of what happened during the frontier years in Tasmania. Critical scholars will tell you that creative writers can always find ways of blaming the victims for their suffering, and J.E. Calder's 1874 account of the "Wars of Extirpation" provided a typical anthropological account for audiences in Great Britain and Ireland who wanted to know how the "habits of the Native tribes of Tasmania" had contributed to their disappearance.[92] Basing his analysis on what he called "authentic official documents" Calder proceeded to lay out for avid readers how the Colonial Secretary's archives—that contained some "seventeen large volumes of manuscript papers"—were filled with prejudicial information that was "almost always on the side of the blacks" in official narrations of the "long quarrel between the two races."[93] Calder, unlike the reformists who raised questions about the wisdom of colonial segregation or Aboriginal reconciliation wanted to tell a very different story.

Calder's purportedly scientific account looked suspiciously like many settler extirpation narratives. In his rendition of affairs Calder claimed that he came across the earlier commentary on the need for protection of the Tasmanian Aborigines and that he worried that "official" accounts did not present a fair account of what really happened during, and after, the Black Wars. In an essay that still reads as if he simply sutured together rhetorical fragments from settler newspapers and local accounts Calder purported to show how those who actually conducted ethnographic studies of the Tasmanian Aborigines possessed the real local knowledge of what had happened in this colony. He juxtaposed these ethnographic insights with the claims that were used by British authorities who patronizingly ordered around the local colonial magistrates. The colonial victims, in Calder's telling of the tale, were the settlers and not necessarily the Aborigines.

Calder was supposed to be presented an objective ethnographic study of the Tasmanians, but many portions of his 1874 account read like something out of James Fenimore Cooper's *Last of the Mohicans*, in that his rendition is filled with discussions of how the settlers and their homesteads were under constant threats of attack from the "savage" or the "black assailant" who was a "crafty enemy."[94] Calder's narration included stories about how Aborigines avoided pitched battles as they perfidiously attacked the "solitary hut of the stock-keeper, or the hapless traveler whom he met in the bush."[95]

Like many twentieth- and twenty-first-century apologists Calder could explain why relatively few records of some of the *actual settler or traveler casualties* showed up in official records. After all, the "black" attacks were often reported in situations where the "largest number that I read of his [sic] destroying in any one occasion being four persons."[96] Until these "barbarians were reduced to a mere remnant by disease and strife," Calder averred, they "never attacked except in parties of twenty, fifty, a hundred, or even greater numbers," testing the "pluck" of the settlers.[97] This seemed to explain why the British critics of the settlers were supposedly getting the mistaken impression from the abolitionists and others that only a few settlers suffered from Aboriginal raids. Calder was arguing that many attacks on settlers were not chronicled by local journalists.

Calder's 1874 exterminationist text contained fragments that made fun of the 1830s' efforts of George Augustus Robinson, that famous principal "captor" and "protector" who didn't seem to understand the blacks' infatuation with their spear and their waddy (hunting stick). At this point in his narration Calder started to use racial stereotypes and ethnic categorizations that explained how Aborigines' "natural instincts" could not be repressed, and how they fought each other at the same time that they fought the settlers. Moreover, Calder seemed to anticipate some of the arguments that were circulated by those who objected to the killing of Aboriginal women and children by asserting that his ethnographic research disclosed how the black females were instructing their communities on how to act aggressively toward whites. While Calder did mention that some of these women were "purchased" from their husbands or fathers by a "lawless handful of ruffians called sealers," he treated some of this violence as instinctual, atavist revenge that was documented in the "days of the decay." Calder's *animus* toward these "barbarians" was so strong that his selective reading of one Aboriginal Committee Report led him to conclude that it showed the "craft of the savage, and his uniform disposition to treachery in his intercourse with the settlers."[98] He was convinced that his own investigations showed that the Tasmanian Aborigines attacked the settlers in spite of the fact that the whites "had never given them the slightest provocation."[99]

Critical genocide scholars can fairly argue that Calder's "anthropological" account was actually a polemically text that tried to underscore the supposed flaws that existed in "conciliatory" policies toward the Aborigines. Calder used Robinson's diaries and records to argue that Robinson—who "probably never had a shot fired at him"—was writing about tribes that were in existence some 15 or 20 years before Robinson went among them, and Calder claimed that Robinson was speculating about why they had "entirely vanished." Not satisfied with the list of causes for this "decay" Calder wrote about how his readers also needed to take into account the "infecundity" of the Tasmanian women.[100] In theory, if the Tasmanians were disappearing, this had more to do with their lack of civilization than the social agency of any settlers.

This would not be the first or last time that pseudo-scientific commentary on the causes of depopulation and the extirpation of the Tasmanians would be used to deflect blame away from those who dispensed systematic violence in the colonies. All of Calder's writings on Aboriginal "infecundity" provided a patina of scientific cover for the frontier racism of that day and age, where someone like Calder could avoid talking about systematic sealer or settler rape. Instead, Calder could blame the victim, and write about their supposed infidelity, and the barbaric "prostitution" that "vitiates" their power of reproduction. Calder tried to argue that he was not sure about all of this but then he quotes someone named Strzelecki who supposedly stood for the doctrine that the "savage woman, after contamination by the white, is invariably and forever [sic] infertile."[101]

At the same time that Calder dismissed some of Strzelecki's claims about the infanticide perpetrated by aboriginal women he was simultaneously objectifying these Aboriginal women and using them strategically in his conversations about "vanishing" communities, race wars, settler innocence, and the supposed horrors of miscegenation. Like many writers during this period he was interesting in arguing that the "rapid declension" of the Tasmanians had everything to do with the "prevalence of epidemic disorders," their "imprudent" habits, the "climate of Tasmania," and the foolishness of the protectors who worked at places like Bruny Island, Flinders Island, and Hunter Island.[102] Calder went so far as to speculate that the Tasmanian Aborigines may have even had an aversion to something that they ate that was "as much an abomination to the entire race as swine's flesh to the Jew or Musselman."[103] Again, all of this naturalization of the extinction of the Tasmanians appeared in the guise of comparative anthropological insight.

Calder's particular account did not accept the "customary" notion that the "Tasmanian savages" were the "most degraded of the human family" or that they possessed "inferior intelligence," because admitting that would have contradicted the claims that he was making elsewhere in his writings about their nefarious habits and their clever attacks on the settlers. Instead, Calder's own brand of colonial racism provided ample opportunities for the questioning of contemporaries who thought that these "savages" were the "link that connected man with the brutes of the field and the forest."[104] Calder highlighted the prowess of the black Tasmanians, who could use tea-tree materials to put together weapons that were some ten feet long, and these could be thrown with precision from a range of some 60 or 70 yards.[105] This kind of attention to detail not only magnified the dangerousness of the Aborigines—it could also be used to rationalize the disproportionate response that came from violent frontier settlements.

In the second half of his anthropological essay Calder was sure that Aboriginal women not only hated whites but despised their half-caste offspring, and this venomous account indicated that animosities ran so high among these "savages" that their quarrels would not die out "except with the extinction of their enemies."[106] This type of discourse provided just one more rationale for why fighting between white settlers and black Aborigines could characterize as an inevitable race war that led to the natural demise of the Tasmanian Aborigines. In a host of ways, Calder's assessment reflected and refracted some of the tacit colonial knowledge of his era, and this was a popular way of contextualized the "Black Wars."

By 1888 the constant repetition of these types of Social Darwinian explanations for the extirpation of the Tasmanians helped evidence the beneficent nature of local patriots who would soon break away from the Britons and call themselves Australians. For example, in a speech that was presented in front of the Australasian Association for the Advancement of Science in 1888, a Hobart lawyer by the name of James Agnew regaled his listeners with talk of how colonial authorities and scientists, as well as nature and nurture, intervened in the affairs of both "King Billy" and Truganini.[107] Truganani may have been identified as the "last" of the Tasmanians, but William Lanne, also known as King Billy, was said to be one of the "last" of the "full-blooded" male Tasmanian men. While Agnew complained that those who collected King Billy's skull and sent it off to the Museum of the Royal College of Surgeons in London had been fooled into thinking that William Lanne was one of the "pure Tasmanian" aboriginals, Agnew was convinced that "King Bill was not a thorough-bred, having the blood of a New South Wales Aborigine in his veins." While Agnew credited Truganini with helping Mr. Robinson convince suspicious aborigines that they needed to move to Oyster Cove, Agnew nevertheless made fun of her as he recalled how her "idea of religion, like those of her race, was dim and misty."[108]

Deploying the often primitivist and racist language of his day James Agnew explained in his 1888 presentation how authorities who dealt with these "children of the forest" had to use "persuasion" that involved both "tact and courage." He elaborated by noting that even if the remnants of this "tribe" had not been removed to Oyster Cove—a locality that was some an "artificial" environment that was 15 miles south of Hobart—their numbers would still have declined rapidly because of the "constant molestation of all kinds of whites."[109]

These types of arguments echoed the claims that were already circulating on several other continents about the degeneration of the unfit, where American communities talked about the need for reservations for Indians or segregated communities for Blacks during the Jim Crow years.

In Tasmanian contexts these "scientific" addresses served as social and psychological vehicles for explaining why the settlers, the convicts, and the soldiers who once patrolled these lands had not intentionally tried to annihilate the Tasmanian Aborigines. Like many colonizers before and after him Agnew had little trouble treating opinions as facts:

> To readers of the earlier history of Tasmania it is well-known that after disturbing relations, attended with much bloodshed on both sides, had existed for some time between the natives and the white settlers, all that remained of the former were induced to submit themselves to Government. They were afterwards removed to Flinder's Island [sic] …. The new mode of life in fact was unsuited to their habits, nostalgia even came to be a factor in the morality and children ceased to be born. The survivors, forty-five in number, were subsequently removed to Oyster Cove.[110]

There are several reasons why this passage is noteworthy. First of all, note how Agnew can gloss over the asymmetrical power relationships that were a part of this earlier colonial warfare. Instead of talking about potential settler atrocities he mentions that both sides had spilled blood and contributed to what he called "disturbing relations." He then writes as though individuals like William Lanne or Truganini died because of acclimatization problems, and this rhetorical framing deflects attention away from what was happening to the "half-breeds" and others who were having to give way in places like Tasmanian and Victoria. Third, notice how the term "survivor" is reserved for those passive Aborigines who had accepted paternal government aid, a bifurcation that implied that those who did not follow colonial orders were at fault, perhaps contributing to their own demise.

Many portions of Agnew's essay were written as though his evaluation of Truganini's life was going to provide Australians with positive proof of the detrimental effects of Aboriginal nostalgia for lost lands. He goes into great detail explaining how "King Billy" had been one of Truganini's four husbands, thus forming an enthymeme that allows his colonial listeners to infer that these heathens had different ways of conceptualizing proper marital habits. Agnew explains how some Tasmanian aboriginals appear to have added to Trugagini's problems when they objected to the help that she gave Robinson, and they "distressed her by prophesying she would live to be the last of her race."[111] Agnew then proceeds to provide his readers with a litany of evidence that pointed to Truganini's growing sense of foreboding and her melancholy acts as she anticipated her own demise. She was described as passionate, "sulky," attached to her dogs and her tobacco.

To underscore her primitiveness Agnew notes how Trugagini supposedly also enjoyed seeing the pictures that appeared in illustrated London papers. Agnew was sure that she had a "profound repugnance for medicine" and he explained that during the nights before she died she knew she was going to die because she kept having visions of her people. For the sake of posterity, Agnew thanked Mrs. C.E. Newell of Hobart for some of this information, and he explained that he was sending along "photographs of Truganini and Billy Lanny."[112] Visual registers thus provided graphic proof of the veracity of the claims that were being made by Agnew about the real causes of the Tasmanians' demise.

By the time nineteenth-century readers get to the end of Agnew's essay they could fairly conclude that if these Aborigines had left behind those irrational yearning for lost lands—and conceded that whites should own those empty territories—then they could have assimilated and they would have lived longer lives. All of this reinforced the notion that the Tasmanian Aborigines were inventing grievances that did not comport with frontier realities.

Several generations of Tasmanians, other Australians, and British subjects were obsessed with trying to recontextualize the demise of either "King Billy" or Truganini, and interpretations evolved to fit *realpolitik* assimilationist or segregationist needs. For example, during the third quarter of the twentieth century William Crowther would reminisce about how several generations of his relatives owned property on Oyster Cove and how they had once lived next to some of the "last" of the Tasmanians. Crowther, who was writing in 1974 for a museum journal about some of the events that took place some 65 years earlier, wrote an essay that supposedly chronicling the daily habits of the Tasmanian survivors living in Oyster Cove.

Portions of Crowther's 1974 account explained to readers that at one time he had been a collector of skulls, skeletons, and other Aboriginal remains. Crowther's telling of the tale of the "last" of the Tasmanians, unlike other stories of the survival of "half-breeds" that had been circulating for more than half a century, focused on the segregated and the harmonious nature of the relationships that were formed between those who appeared doomed for extinction and the local caretakers, scientists, and British authorities who were doing everything that they could to help during the Aborigines' last days. The personal became political as Crowther wrote about how, when he was growing up, he used to play in the "dilapidated remains of the Reserve Buildings," and he explained how this place had once served as the final home for the "last 45 of the Tasmanian natives" who had been removed from Flinders Island in 1847 in the hopes that they would survive in places like Oyster Cove.

Crowther was a physician, and he couldn't help viewing the demise of the Tasmanians through clinical lenses that recorded their diets, their responses to inclement weather, and their reactions to the presence of the many dignitaries who came to visit them before they died. In what some critical scholars might call his biopolitical or thanatopolitical account Crowther argued that for healthy people who had "definite occupations" Oyster Cove was a place that might have been an ideal choice for the clearing of some land for the "natives." However, in this instance the "ill-starred, depressed, old and idle" Tasmanians were living in some unhealthy surroundings.[113]

Again, Crowther does not focus attention on the *violence that was perpetrated before* the removal of the Tasmanian Aboriginals to Flinders Island or Oyster Cove. His is a tale of imperial beneficence, where the British colonizers and their local subalterns were doing the best that they could to improve the lot of those who were destined to vanish. Crowther wrote sympathetically about the daily requests of Aborigines who liked tobacco and certain food dishes, but he changed the tone of the essay when he told his readers about the "possibility of exhuming bodies at Oyster Cove" during the first decade of the twentieth century.[114]

The guilt-ridden Crowther of 1974 perhaps understood that the earlier generations of settlers saw nothing wrong with the idea of exhuming Tasmanian remains. However, with the passage of time, as he studied the records of the "last few months of the survivors of the Race," Crowther admitted that he was having feelings of "deep regret and dissatisfaction."[115] In spite of these reminisces Crowther wrote as if very few settlers or Britons harbored any ill-will, and he went into great detail explaining why the gentry who traveled to Oyster Cove to see this "final phase of the extinct Tasmanian Race." Who didn't want to get a glimpse of the last of the Tasmanians? Voyeurism becomes a part of a benevolent settler politics of pity.

Crowther's 1974 account read like a meticulous log of the weekly, monthly, or yearly recordings of the activities of those who tried to save the remnants of the Tasmanians, yet it looked nothing like the account that would be produced some 34 years later by an influential genocide scholar. Tony Barta wrote an essay where he averred that Parliamentary members knew about the displacement of the Aborigines and the near extinction of the Tasmanians. He admitted that British decision-makers took steps, "however inadequate," to avert this disaster,[116] but he implied that this belated response accomplished little. Barta then opined that British colonial and imperial authorities knew that settler colonization relationships "were endemic to colonization" and he remained convinced that the use of a "short-lived Protectorate" did not absolve the British in London from blame. Their "larger intentions"—that were demonstrated by their "get rich" wool schemes in Tasmania or in the colony of Victoria—were believed to provide the type of evidence that led him to take the unpopular stance that genocide had been committed.[117]

Barta's brand of critical genocidal argumentation did not sit well with more traditional scholars, but it could be argued that he was extending some of the arguments of his predecessors—like Melville—and taking them to their logical conclusion. Years before Barta would write these words there would be others who started to leave fragments that would become a part of what would later be called the "Tasmanian genocide hypothesis."

Before World War II the older journalistic debates about the "protection," "reconciliation," or "extirpation" of the Tasmanian Aborigines temporarily receded from scholarly and public view, but some of this started to change with the publication of Clive Turnbull's *Black War* in 1948.[118] The subtitle of Turnbull's book—the *Extermination of the Tasmanian Aborigines*—not only signaled that he believed in the existence of an ethnic group known as the Tasmanians but it also invited readers to review the causes of their demise. Not surprisingly, given post-World War II sensibilities, portions of Turnbull's book compared the Aboriginal extermination with the Nazi perpetration of the Holocaust, but it would be decades before these types of comparisons would resonate with some academicians and public audiences.

Talk of Tasmanian Genocides and Calls for Apologias and Other Forms of Postcolonial Redress, 1975–2018

Turnbull's book garnered some attention, but members of transcontinental publics needed to be in a mood for change before paradigms can shift, and this gradually happened. Lyndall Ryan's book, *The Aboriginal Tasmanians* (1981), would be used by descendants of those who had survived the massacres to tell the world that the Tasmanians had not disappeared. Passages in her book raised eyebrows when they mentioned that Aborigines were the victims of a "conscious policy of genocide."[119]

Scholars in Australia, New Zealand, and other interested communities critiqued the work of Turnbull and Ryan and other authors as they argued back and forth about the relevant theories, methods, and conclusions that should be reached in disputation about various genocidal hypotheses. Was Tony Barta right in 1987 when he claimed that the British settlement of Australia was an endeavor that was conducted in ways that ensured that Australia would be a "nation founded on genocide"?[120] In his *Fate of a Free People* Henry Reynolds—considered by some to be an apolitical researcher—responded to those types of accusations by emphasizing the point that perhaps this was not the best way to characterize the demographic losses that were suffered during "a war."[121] More than a dozen years later, A. Dirk Moses tried to present another balanced view in the pages of the *Journal of Genocide Research* when he averred that perhaps the officials in the colony were trying to lead with a "restraining hand" but were having to deal with "radical exterminatory sentiments."[122]

What is intriguing to note here in my genealogical reading of Antipodean disputation is that it would not be the Tasmanian exterminationist debates that would capture the attention of large numbers of scholars or readers during this period. A few read the work of Ryan or Barta, but it would be the labor of the members of the government inquiry on the "separation of Aboriginal and Torres Strait Islander Children" that would resonate with public readers. This report, released in 1997, helped advance the cause of those who wanted to prevent the sanitizing of Australian pasts.[123] This 1997 government inquiry included commentary on the removal of some 100,000 indigenous children so that they could be assimilated into the broader "white" culture, and authors of the inquiry report concluding that these particular acts could "properly be labeled 'genocidal.'"[124]

The public disputation that began with these 1990s' debates about the "stolen" generations morphed into what where called the Australian "history wars" as other scholars started to converse about various continuity theories or paradigm shifts that might take into account comparative Holocaust studies[125] or work on colonial genocides and the "Tasmanian genocide hypothesis." In 2001, Henry Reynolds, a writer known for sympathizing with some indigenous causes, nevertheless published a book whose title says it all: *An Indelible Stain? The Question of Genocide in Australia's History.*[126] Reynolds book was considered to be canonical by those scholars and members of the public who refused to believe that there was any stain that had anything to do with denialism. Yes, settlers had been involved in a few massacres, but nothing on the scale of anything like the World War II Holocaust.

One influential skeptic of the Tasmanian genocide thesis, Norman J.B. Plomley, was willing to admit that before the British settlers arrived in Tasmania in 1803 there may have been between 4000 and 6000 indigenous Tasmanians, but he goes on to use a multi-causal analysis to explain that it had been disease and other factors, as well as settler abuse, that led to the demise of the Tasmanians. In Promley's configuration of what he called the "Aboriginal/Settler clash" the Aboriginals did not need to be treated as some passive, defenseless victims of some intentional genocide. Instead, like Calder before him, he characterized the Aborigines as empowered social agents who fought in a bloody war to remove the settlers from their lands.[127] This type of framing resonated with many British and Australian academics, newspaper writers, and laypersons.[128]

During the first decade of the twenty-first century the "history wars" in Australia became more heated when defenders of the genocide thesis critiqued the work that would be produced by the more conservative authors who published their research in outlets like *Quadrant*. Ben Kiernan, for example, could complain about the "cover-up" and "denial" that came when obstinate Australians and other scholars, supposedly intent on preserving an untarnished image of Australian settlement, still refused to revise their histories on the basis of new information or historiographies.[129] Kiernan's target would be the Australian scholars who wanted to preserve beneficent images of British imperialism that could be displayed as examples of "benign paternalism."[130]

To provide readers with more examples of how historical facts can be (re)viewed through patriotic or apologetic prisms, note the way that Professor Keith Windschuttle, in his *Fabrication* (2002) ended up arguing that during the Black War twice as many "whites were killed as blacks."[131] Windschuttle tried to prove that hundreds, not thousands, of Tasmanian Aborigines had been killed during some of these early frontier conflicts, and he used arguments about disease and the abuse of women to argue that this helped account for recorded demographic declines. Windschuttle's supporters agreed with his assessment that a review of the predominate philosophical and religious beliefs of the times would have *restrained the hands* of those who might have been tempted to annihilate the Tasmanians.

Windschuttle's efforts were lauded by conservatives and others who objected to the idea that Australian settlement had anything to do with genocides. Windschuttle told reporters in 2002 that if "Australians of Aboriginal and European descent are to look one another straight in the eye, they have to face the truth about their mutual history, not rely upon mythologies designed to create an edifice of black victimhood and white guilt."[132] This argumentative line would be used during twenty-first-century disputes over land development, Aboriginal title, and the preservation of indigenous heritage.[133]

Windshuttle's arguments need to be analyzed by critical genocide scholars because I sense that in the coming decades they will be redeployed by stakeholders who have little interest in hearing about the need for future land distribution, reparations for indigenous communities, or the repatriation of Tasmanian remains. Windshuttle's critiques of colonial genocides and Australian historiography are going to resonate with descendants of former colonizers who do not want to apologize for alleged colonial abuses.

It is no coincidence that Windshuttle helps establish his own credibility by asking whether it is possible that individuals who read the journals of

George August Robinson, and those who treat them as the gospel, were being duped into believing the "myth" of the Tasmanian genocide. Instead of relying on what he considers to be "secondary sources"—the materials that appear in the newspapers of the 1830s—he turns to what he views as the "primary" materials that can be found in official archives. Windschuttle, in an essay entitled the "Fabrication of Aboriginal History," seemed to conflate the *ontological existence* of these large-scale atrocities that may have been committed against the Tasmanian Aborigines with the *epistemic evidence of our recordings* of these same events. By placing the burden of proof on the shoulders of his academic adversaries he could debunk the claims of those who defended the Tasmanian genocide thesis.[134]

Part of the populist appeal of Windschuttle's efforts stems from the strategic ways he sets out the ground rules for this disputation. He begins by assuming that Australian and Tasmanian governments should be viewed as innocent parties that have nothing to do with these atrocity charges, and then he asks his critics to make out a prima facie *case* against the settlers and the colonial authorities. For example, Windschuttle attacked Lyndall Ryan for her citation of the *Hobart Town Courier* as a source of reliable information about atrocities that may have been committed against Aborigines in 1826 when that outlet only started publication October of 1827. At the same time, he faulted Ryan for using Robinson's journal in order to document the hundreds of Aboriginals who may have been killed. In one typical passage Windschuttle averred:

> Robinson's diaries record a total of only 188 aborigines killed by whites, and many of them are dubious claims. [Lyndall] Ryan says that the documentary evidence shows 280 Aborigines were "recorded shot" and that the unrecorded killings would bring the total to 700. However, she provides no sources for these figures. Brian Plomley did a survey in 1992 but could find records of only 109 Aborigines killed. I could find records for only 120.[135]

The operative logic of this archival literalism was clear: if those who were advancing the Tasmanian genocide thesis were relying on the same sources, and if they were collectively making so many historiographic mistakes in their discussions of what happened during the 1820s, then it must have been the case that only a few hundred aboriginals were shot by white settlers or soldiers. Windschuttle similarly accused Rhys Jones of misinterpreting the materials from the 1830 Committee Into Aboriginal Affairs in ways that purportedly led Jones to invent some of the "latter atrocities."[136]

Windschuttle's approach resonated with many Australians, New Zealanders, and local Tasmanians in places like Hobart because he seemed to be debunking the promoters of the genocide thesis at the same time that he cited the "real" evidence that came from rival settler newspapers that made fun of the conciliators who talked and wrote about atrocities. An editor by the name of Robert Lathorp Murray, for example, got into a heated discursive battle with James Ross, the editor of the *Hobart Town Courier*. Ross worried in 1830 about the actual extent of the violence, but Windschuttle cites a passage from Murray:

> No doubt that they are enabled to commit many atrocities, most frequently by the exercise of that cunning by which all savages are distinguished, but to talk of six dozen miserable creatures, and never was a large body seen assembled than 72, driving us from this room, is of course a joke.[137]

By 2003 Keith Windschuttle was able to argue that in spite of its "infamous reputation" Van Diemen's Land was "host to nothing that resembled genocide, which requires murderous intent against a whole race of people." He argued that the 1830 Black Line was not some act of "ethnic cleansing," but was instead an organized attempt by the settler districts to get two of the nine Aboriginal tribes on the island to move "to uninhabited country from which they could no longer assault white households."[138] Clearly Windschuttle did see any major problem with what could be interpreted as peaceful dispossession, segregation, and forced removal of populations. He, like many other Australian historians, could use legalistic definitions of genocide to help police the traditional genocidal canons.

Windschuttle may have sincerely believed that he was setting the historical record straight, and yet critical genealogists could point out that he was simply recirculating a variant of the apologetic arguments that had been co-produced by the journalists of the nineteenth century. Those journalists spilled a great deal of ink defending the convicts, the settlers, and the sealers who waged race war against the Aborigines, and now their old claims were being recirculated in the early twenty-first-century Australian history wars.

Ironically, many of the academic conclusions that Windschuttle claimed were derived from primary sources were echoing many of the ideological rationales for "extirpation" that were produced by generations of journalists living in settler communities. Moreover, this supposed iron-clad case for genocide skepticism or revisionism can be de-territorialized in ways that highlight the ideological nature of Windschuttle's narrations. Note, for example, how Windshuttle's account is filled with a host of contestable claims:

> The truth is that there was nothing on the Aborigines' side that resembled frontier warfare, patriotic struggle or systematic resistance of any kind. The so-called "Black War" was a minor crime wave by two Europeanised black bushrangers, followed by an outbreak of robbery, assault and murder by tribal Aborigines. All of the evidence of the time, on both the white and black sides of the frontier, was that their principal objective was to acquire flour, tea, sugar and bedding, objects that to them were European luxury goods.[139]

It seemed as though Windschuttle was convinced that his own preferred historiographic way of analyzing texts led him to the "truth" that this "minor crime" looked nothing like any large-scale genocide. He could compartmentalize and isolate historical incidents to counter those who found genocidal intents, patterns, or structures.

If Windschuttle had stopped there it would have been controversial enough, but then he started to assemble together a host of arguments that seemed to have been taken straight from nineteenth- and twentieth-century colonial accounts that were based on a welter of problematic ethnographic, eugenical, or acclimatization assumptions. Windschuttle, for example, recirculated the racial discourse of an earlier age as he argued that the "full-blood Tasmanian Aborigines did die out in the nineteenth century," but then he wanted the readers of "the Fabrication of Aboriginal History" essay to believe that it had been the "10,000 years of isolation" that left them vulnerable to diseases like influence, pneumonia, or tuberculosis. Again, note how Windschuttle sounds like Calder when he writes that the Aborigines suffered extinction because "they traded and prostituted their women to convict stockmen and sealers to such an extent that they lost the ability to reproduce themselves."[140]

This type of blaming the victim reprised the arguments of nineteenth-century "ethnographers" like Calder, and yet given cultural anxieties we can readily understand the public interest in legitimating historical research that claims that the colonizers were "responsible for killing only 120 of the original inhabitants." This strategic rhetorical framing treats Van Diemen's Land as the place where a colonial encounter took place that spilled the "least indigenous blood" of all that "was deliberately shed."[141]

A form of prideful exceptionalism creeps into historical disputation as Tasmanian or Australian settler colonialism can be compared to more violent conquests.

The Britons who settled Tasmanian end up looking nothing like the Belgian colonizers of the Congo Free State, the French in Algeria, or the Spanish forces in Morocco who tried to subdue the Berbers. Here there is no "stain" to be removed by anyone (see Reynolds), and the avid reader of Windschuttle's work has no reason to take the next step and consider Tasmanian restorative justice claims.

These apologetic or revisionist approaches to colonial genocide—that often focused on the need for critics to provide some demonstrative proof of intent—were critiqued by a variety of neo-liberal and radical observers who wanted to see more structuralist, functionalist, or materialist explanations for Van Diemen's violence. As Shayne Breen would note in 2011:

> A colonial genocide refers to both process and outcome: the indisputable fact is that the Tasmanian Aborigines all but disappeared as a direct result of colonial occupation by the British. They disappeared as a the result of an accretion of actions, some of which were clearly crimes, including the abduction of their women and children, the killing of Aboriginal men by colonists convicts, and the military, and a war of extermination sanctioned by the colonial governor but which Colonial Secretary George Murray and a small number of colonists regarded as organized murder … the insistence that unambiguous intent to exterminate must exist for genocide to occur rests on a narrow legalistic definition of genocide.[142]

Professor Breen went on to argue that regardless of what we call the "particular action" that had an "exterminatory impact" the British government "intended to take Aboriginal land fully aware of the likely outcome."[143]

Yet supporters of writers like Windschuttle might respond that Breen's work does not provide any prima facie case of genocidal intent that would be recognized by those who are familiar with the UN Genocide Convention provisions. A popular technique that is used by some historians and others who treat talk of the "genocide" of the Tasmanian as more of a "theory" than an existential reality involves the use of strategic historiographic strategies that demand that critical genocide scholars *account for the names or similar evidencing* of the dead before we talk of tens of thousands of massacred aborigines.[144] Henry Reynolds, for example, in his 2014 foreword of Clements' *The Black War*, argues that between 1925 and 1831 "close to 200 Britons and 1000 Aborigines" died violently in Tasmania's Black War.[145] Yet dying during a "war," as Lemkin and others have noted, does not automatically mean that one has provided evidence of genocidal intent.

Focusing on "war," and clinging to narrow interpretations of Lemkin's work or UN definitions, served as ways of explaining Aboriginal loss of life without having to concede anything about cultural genocide or indigenocide. This was the type of bloody conflict that Russell McGregor has described as being one where reports indicated, that least during some portions of "The Black War," that the Aboriginal Tasmanians "gave as bloodily as they got."[146] The work of Nicholas Clements,[147] which includes analyses of settlers accounts of being stalked and killed by Aborigines, can be used by those who want to argue that the Aboriginals were not "the helpless victims of all-powerful colonizers but effective fighters who struck terror in their adversaries and were defeated only by weight of numbers."[148]

In 2014 Tom Lawson added a new twist to some of these genocidal debates and history wars when he linked these Tasmanian disputes to other historical and contemporary remembrances in the United Kingdom. One of his books, entitled, *The Last Man, a British Genocide in Tasmania*, challenged the "assumed separation of a destructive, indeed genocidal, Empire from its British home."[149] What if British imperialists in London were also culpable parties?

Conclusion

Like other cases of disputation about the inherent violence of settler colonialism or the beneficence of confrontational, segregationist, or assimilationist rhetorics the debates about the Tasmanian genocide are not going to go away any time soon. "Despite over 170 years of debate over who or what was responsible for this near extinction" in Tasmania, noted Professor Madley in 2008, "no consensus exists on its origins, process, or whether or not it was genocide."[150] Madley's own position was that a "culture of terror" had shaped the early "colonists' lives, psyches, and behavior,"[151] and that the release of thousands of convicts only exacerbated the problems of local towns and farms that had to cope with multiple sources of terror. While he thought that more "regional studies" might help answer Tony Barta's older 1987 question regarding Australia's founding as a genocidal nation, he thought that there was enough historical evidence to support the claim that "under British rule," Tasmania had once been a "site of genocide."[152]

During the first decade of the twentieth century Aunt Ida West—born on the Aboriginal Reserve at Cape Barren Island—would lead ceremonies like the Hobart Walk for Reconciliation in 2000 that brought together some 25,000 people so that they could gather together, march, and talk about topics such as the meaning of real decolonization or reconciliation.[153] Some early twenty-first-century marches that were led by Aboriginal Tasmanians were intended to retrace the steps of those who crossed the old Black Line at places like Three Thumbs. Penelope Edmonds contends that the Three Thumbs crossing and other acts of commemorative remembrances are "performances" that "constituted a radical form of localized Aboriginal countermapping, where each site of violence was physically visited, ceremonies performed," and "landscapes resacralized, or returned to the sacred."[154] Oftentimes the scholarly work on the Tasmanian genocide thesis would be used by activists to help legitimate some of their restorative justice claims.

Does the adoption of a critical genocidal vantage point help us assess whether Professor Moses is right when he argues that if many of the Britons did not "consciously" will the annihilation of the Tasmanians, *their actions* spoke volumes in that they "silently" were "condoning" what was happening all around them?[155] After all, they consistently defended the appropriation of more and more land at the same time that they tried to use segregationist or annihilationist framings of the demise of the Tasmanians. Should that governmental involvement be used by Aboriginal activists who ask for governmental apologies, genocidal acknowledgment, or the return of Aboriginal lands?

I stand with those critical genocide scholars who have argued that actions, and not just words or intentions, can be used to evidence the perpetration of indigenocides or genocides, and that the very attempt to systematically replace the Tasmanians with colonizing Britons should give pause to those who would summarily dismiss these arguments.

Notes

1. Some of those who will have laid the scholarly groundwork for the inclusion of the Tasmanian genocide in those traditional genocidal canons include Ann Curthoys, "Genocide in Tasmania: The History of An Idea,' in *Empire, Colony, Genocide: Conquest, Occupation and Subaltern Resistance in World History*, edited by Dirk Moses (New York: Berghahn Books, 2010), 229–252; Tony Barta, "Relations of Genocide: Land and Lives in the Colonization of Australia," in *Genocide and the Modern Age:*

Etiology and Case Studies of Mass Death, edited by Isidor Wallimann and Michael N. Dobkowski (Westport, CT: Greenwood Press, 1987), 237–251; John Docker, "A Plethora of Intentions: Genocide, Settler Colonialism and Historical Consciousness in Australia and Britain," *The International Journal of Human Rights* 19, no. 1 (2015): 74–89; Thomas James Rogers and Stephen Bain, "Genocide and Frontier Violence in Australia," *Journal of Genocide Research* 18, no. 1 (2016): 83–100.
2. Penelope Edmonds, "'Our History Is Not the Last Word': Sorry Day at Risdon Cove and 'Black Line' Survival Ceremony, Tasmania," in *Settler Colonialism and (Re)conciliation* (London: Palgrave Macmillan, 2016), 126–219.
3. Nick Brodie, *The Vandemonian War: The Secret History of Britain's Tasmanian Invasion* (Sydney: Hardie Grant, 2017).
4. Benjamin Madley, "Command, Control and Genocide: A Review of *The Vandemonian War*," *Journal of Genocide Research* 20, no. 3 (2018): 467–471, 470–471.
5. Güenter Lewy, "Documents and Discussions: Reply to Tony Barta, Norbert Finzsch and David Stannard," *Journal of Genocide Research* 10, no. 2 (2008): 307.
6. Henry Reynolds, *An Indelible Stain? The Question of Genocide in Australia's History* (Melbourne: Viking, 2001).
7. Helen Davison, "John Howard: There Was No Genocide Against Indigenous Australians," *The Guardian*, last modified September 22, 2014, https://www.theguardian.com/world/2014/sep/22/john-howard-there-was-no-genocide-against-indigenous-australians
8. Madeline Hayman-Reber, "The Black War: Tasmania Still Torn by Its History," *Special Broadcasting Services*, last modified April 20, 2018, paragraphs 9–18, https://www.sbs.com.au/nitv/nitv-news/article/2018/04/19/black-war-tasmania-still-torn-its-history
9. Kristyn Harman, "Explainer: The Evidence for the Tasmanian Genocide," *The Conversation*, last modified January 17, 2018, paragraphs 2, 4, https://theconversation.com/explainer-the-evidence-for-the-tasmanian-genocide-86828
10. Edmonds, "'Our History Is Not the Last Word,'" 129.
11. For an excellent overview of some of the different lexicons that would be used to describe what we call the "genocide" or the "indigenocide" of the Tasmanians, see Curthoys, "Genocide in Tasmania," 229–252.
12. Ann Curthoys, "Genocide in Tasmania," 229.
13. Edmonds, "'Our History Is Not the Last Word,'" 136.
14. *Sydney Morning Herald* Staff, "Our History, Not Rewritten but Put Right," *The Sydney Morning Herald*, November 25, 2002, paragraph 2, https://www.smh.com.au/opinion/our-history-not-rewritten-but-put-right-20021125-gdfv47.html

15. William R. Price, "Overcoming the Myth of Extinction: The Path Toward Heritage Rights for the Tasmanian Aboriginals," *Heritage & Society* 10, no. 1 (2017): 68–90, 68.
16. See Richard H. King and Dan Stone, *Hannah Arendt and the Uses of History: Imperialism, Nation, Race and Genocide* (New York: Berghahn Books, 2008).
17. Raphaël Lemkin, "Tasmania" [edited by Ann Curthoys], *Patterns of Prejudice* 39, no. 2 (1996): 170–196, 178.
18. Edmonds, "'Our History Is Not the Last Word,'" 144.
19. For an example of the hagiography that swirls around Lemkin's work see the 2005 special issue of the *Journal of Genocide Research*, From the Guest Editors, "Raphael Lemkin: the 'Founder of the United Nation's Genocide Convention' As a Historian of Mass Violence," *Journal of Genocide Research* 7, no. 4 (2005): 447–452.
20. Patrick Wolfe, "Forum Essay: Land, Labor, and Difference: Elementary Structures of Race," *American Historical Review* 106, no. 3 (June 2001): 866–905.
21. Ibid., 871.
22. See, Douglas Irvin-Erickson, *Raphael Lemkin and the Concept of Genocide* (Philadelphia: University of Pennsylvania Press, 2017).
23. For an example of an academic work that shares my interest in deploying critical genealogical or Foucauldian critiques of debates over the Tasmanian genocide, see Jess Shipway, *Scars of the Archive, Visions of Place: Genocide and Modernity in Tasmania* (Hobart: University of Tasmania, 2005).
24. We need to treat Lemkin's texts as just some of the influential shards of memory that are a part of dense ideological *epistemes* that have been circulating since the first half of the nineteenth century. These were historical periods when physical anthropologists, diplomats, journalists, and others left us competing interpretations of how to respond to what would later be called the Social Darwinian "extirpation" of the Tasmanians.
25. Michel Foucault, "Nietzsche, Genealogy, History," in *Language, Counter-Memory, Practice: Selected Essays and Interviews by Michael Foucault* (1971: Ithaca: Cornell University Press, 1977), 139.
26. As readers might imagine there are those who say there is no reason to say sorry. See Andrew Bold, "We Should Not Be Saying Sorry to Aborigines," *Herald Sun*, last modified January 29, 2008, https://www.heraldsun.com.au/news/opinion/we-should-not-be-saying-this/news-story/
27. James Bonwick, *The Last of the Tasmanians; or, The Black War of Van Diemen's Land* (London: Sampson Low, 1870).
28. Lemkin, "Tasmania," 171. There are variant spellings of this land, sometimes called Van Dieman's Land and at other times called Van Diemen's Land.

29. Professor Bromley is one of those who estimated that somewhere between 4000 and 6000 Tasmanians may have died during British settlement. Norman J. B. Plomley, *The Aboriginal/Settler Clash in Van Diemen's Land: 1803–1831* (Hobart: University of Tasmania, 1992), 10. For similar figures see Henry Reynolds, *Fate of a Free People: A Radical Reexamination of the Tasmanian Wars* (Ringwood: Victoria Penguin Books, Australia, 1995), 4. Some of those who have proposed that we adopt larger figures of Aborigines' morality rates often depend on what are called "precontact" Aboriginal Tasmanian population statistics. David Davies, for example, asserts that in 1803 it was possible that the population of Van Diemen's Land was in the neighborhood of 15,000. David Davies, *The Last of the Tasmanians* (Sydney: Williams Collins, 1973), 120.
30. "Minority literatures" is the name Gilles Deleuze and Felix Guattari give to those marginalized interpretations that are presented by the disempowered or others who contest dominant readings of texts. Gilles Deleuze and Felix Guattari, *Kafka: Toward a Minor Literature*, translated by Dana Polan (Minneapolis: University of Minnesota Press, 1986). Critical scholars have appropriated some of this language in their studies of the contingent, partial, and motivated nature of colonial or imperial texts.
31. Shayne Breen, "Extermination, Extinction, Genocide: British Colonialism and Tasmanian Aborigines," in *Forgotten Genocides: Oblivion, Denial, and Memory*, edited by René Lemarchand (Philadelphia: University of Pennsylvania Press, 2011), 70.
32. Edmonds, "'Our History Is Not the Last Word,'" 126.
33. Anna Johnston, "George August Robinson, the 'Great Conciliator': Colonial Celebrity and Its Postcolonial Aftermath," *Postcolonial Studies* 12, no. 2 (2009): 153–152, 170.
34. Benjamin Madley, "From Terror to Genocide: Britain's Tasmanian Penal Colony and Australia's History Wars," *Journal of British Studies* 47, no. 1 (January 2008): 77–106, 78. For a more comparative study see Benjamin Madley, "Patterns of Frontier Genocide 1803–1910: The Aboriginal Tasmanians, the Yuki of California, and the Herero of Namibia," *Journal of Genocide Research* 6, no. 2 (June 2004): 167–192. For examples of how what happened in Tasmanian has become a part of many Australian and British "history wars" see Stuart Macintyre and Anna Clark, *The History Wars* (Melbourne: Melbourne University Press, 2003). For an illustration of continued interest critiquing academic interest in the genocidal dimensions of these history wars, see Theodore Dalrymple, "Why Intellectuals Like Genocide," *New England Review* (July, 2007), http://www.newenglishreview.org/Theodore_Dalrymple/Why_Intellectuals_Like_Genocide/
35. See Patrick Wolfe's analysis of some of this deviousness. Wolfe, "Land, Labor, and Difference."
36. Rogers and Stephen Bain, "Genocide and Frontier Violence," 85.

37. Raymond Evans and Bill Thorpe, “Indigenocide and the Massacre of Aboriginal History,” *Overland* (2011): 21–39.
38. John Dawson, “Van Demonisation: The Revival of the Tasmanian Genocide Thesis,” *Quadrant* 52, no. 11 (November 2008): 48–53.
39. Ibid., 53.
40. John Dawson, *Washout: On the Academic Response to the Fabrication of Aboriginal History* (Sydney: Macleay Press, 2004).
41. For the attempted mainstreaming of some of these ideas see John Dawson, “The Truth Wars,” *Australian Broadcast Network*, last modified March 7, 2005, https://www.abc.net.au/radionational/programs/archived/perspective/john-dawson/3443660
42. William E. L. H. Crowther, “The Final Phase of the Extinct Tasmanian Race, 1847–1876,” *Records of the Queen Victoria Museum* 49 (1974): 1–34, 2.
43. Lieutenant Governor Arthur, quoted in Madley, “From Terror to Genocide,” 83.
44. Keith Windschuttle, “The Myths of Frontier Massacres in Australian History,” *Quadrant* 44, no. 11 (November 2000): 17–24.
45. Johnston, “George August Robinson,” 170.
46. Herman Merivale, *Lectures on Colonization and Colonies, Delivered Before the University of Oxford in 1839, 1840 & 1841*, 2 Volumes (London: Longman, Brown, Green, and Longmans, 1842), II, 150.
47. Ibid., 153.
48. Edmonds, “‘Our History Is Not the Last Word,’” 138.
49. Ibid.
50. Plomley, *The Aboriginal/Settler Clash*, 10–29; Reynolds, *Fate of a Free People*, 3–4.
51. Madley, “Patterns of Frontier Genocide,” 170.
52. See A Dirk Moses, “An Antipodean Genocide? The Origins of the Genocidal Moment in the Colonization of Australia,” *Journal of Genocide Research* 2, no. 1 (March 2000): 89–106.
53. Plomley, *The Aboriginal/Settler Clash*, 25.
54. Robert Hughes, *The Fatal Shore* (New York: Alfred A. Knopf, 1987), 371.
55. James Ross, *The Settler in Van Diemen’s Land* (1836; Melbourne, Marsh Walsh, 1975), 17.
56. Madley, “From Terror to Genocide,” 83. For contemporary examples of critiques of these lashings, see James Backhouse, *Extracts from Letters of James Backhouse Whilst Engaged in a Religious Visit to Van Diemen’s Land, New South Wales, and South Africa*, 2 volumes (London: Harvey and Darton, 1841).
57. Thomas Lempriere, *The Penal Settlements of Early Van Diemen’s Land* (1839; Tasmania: Royal Society of Tasmania, 1954), 60.
58. Madley, “From Terror to Genocide,” 85.

59. See Patrick Wolfe, "Settler Colonialism and the Elimination of the Native," *Journal of Genocide Research* 8, no. 4 (December 2006): 387–409.
60. Bonwick, *Last of the Tasmanians*, 61. The notion of the "last" of the Tasmanians would be a topic that appealed to those wanting to keep visual records of these events as well. See, for example, the 1978 Australian documentary, Tom Haydon, *The Last Tasmanian*: A Story of Genocide (Avalon Beach, New South Wales: Maxwell's Collection, 1982).
61. Madley, "From Terror to Genocide," 86.
62. Ibid., 87. For other discussions of other colonial origins of similar annihilations rhetorics, see Ben Kiernan, *Blood and Soil: A World History of Genocide and Extermination from Sparta to Darfur* (New Haven, CT: Yale University Press, 2007).
63. Lieutenant Governor Arthur to Secretary Sir George Murray, November 20, 1830, *Correspondence Between Lieutenant Governor Arthur and His Majesty's Secretary of State for the Colonies, on the Subject of the Military Operations Lately Carried Out Against the Aboriginal Inhabitants of Van Diemen's Land* (Cambridge: House of Commons, Parliamentary Papers, 1831), 60, quoted in Madley, "From Terror to Genocide," 87.
64. Ibid.
65. Plomley, *Aboriginal/Settler Clash*, 5; Madley, "From Terror to Genocide," 88.
66. Madley, "From Terror to Genocide," 90.
67. Ibid., 91.
68. Ibid.
69. Lyndall Ryan, *The Aboriginal Tasmanians* (St. Leonards: Allen & Unwin, 1996), 85.
70. Andrew Darby, "More Than 1000 Died in Tasmanian War, Says Historian," *The Sydney Morning Herald*, last modified April 28, 2012, https://www.smh.com.au/national/more-than-1000-died-in-tasmanian-war-says-historian-20120427-1xq5p.html
71. For an example of attempts to provide contrapuntal or counterhistorical readings of Tasmanian histories and memories see Leonie Stevens, *"Me Write Myself": The Free Aboriginal Inhabitants of Van Diemen's Land at Wybaleena, 1832–47* (Clayton: Monash University Publishing, 2017).
72. Madley, "Patterns of Frontier Genocide," 171.
73. For a critique of Robinson's efforts see Ashley Riley Sousa, "'They Will Be Hunted Down Like Wild Beasts and Destroyed': A Comparative Study of Genocide in California and Tasmania," *Journal of Genocide Research* 6, no. 2 (2004): 193–209.
74. See Tony Barta, "Mr. Darwin's Shooters: On Natural Selection and the Naturalizing of Genocide," *Patterns of Prejudice* 39, no. 2 (2005): 116–137.

75. David Burn, *A Picture of Van Diemen's Land* (Hobart: Cat & Fiddle Press, 1973), 22.
76. Backhouse, *Extracts*, I: 15.
77. Henry Melville, *The History of the Island of Van Diemen's Land from the Year 1824 to 1835* (1835: Sydney: Halstead Press, 1965), 31; Madley, "Patterns of Frontier Genocide," 172.
78. Jeni Thornley, "Race Wars Written Out of Australian History," *Jen Thornley Documentary*, last modified April 23, 2007, http://jenithorn-leydoco.blogspot.com/2007/04/race-wars-written-out-of-australian.html?m=0
79. Henry Saxelby Melville, *The History of Van Diemen's Land: from the Year 1824 to 1835*, edited by George Mackaness (1836: Hobart: Horwitz-Grahame, 1965), 56–57.
80. John West, *The History of Tasmania* (Launceston: Henry Dowling, 1852), II, 18. For an example of another account from these same years see Thomas Atkins, *Reminiscences of Twelve Years' Residence in Tasmania and New South Wales, Norfolk Island and Moreton Bay; Calcutta, Madras and Cape Town; The United States of America; and the Canadas* (Malvern, Australia: Advertiser, 1869).
81. Shayne Breen, "Extermination, Extinction, Genocide," 84.
82. Edmonds, "'Our History Is Not the Last Word,'" 147.
83. For an overview of varies responses to the Black Line see Lyndall Ryan, "The Black Line in Van Diemen's Land: Success or Failure," *Journal of Australian Studies* 37, no. 1 (2013): 3–18.
84. Ibid., 84.
85. Russell McGregor, "Review: *The Black War: Fear, Sex and Resistance in Tasmania*," *Australian Journal of Politics and History* 60, no. 3 (2014): 466–467, 466.
86. Alex Tyrrell, *A Sphere of Benevolence: The Life of Joseph Orton, Wesleyan Methodist Missionary, 1795–1842* (Melbourne: State Library of Victoria, 1993), 140.
87. Tyrell, *A Sphere of Benevolence*, 141; Tony Barta, "'They Appear to Vanish from the Face of the Earth.' Aborigines and the European Project in Australia Felix," *Journal of Genocide Research* 10, no. 4 (2008): 519–539, 538.
88. Henry Reynolds, "Genocide in Tasmania?" in A. Dirk Moses, "Genocide and Settler Society in Australian History," in *Genocide and Settler Society: Frontier Violence and Stolen Indigenous Children in Australian History*, edited by A. Dirk Moses (New York: Berghahn Books, 2004), 147: Madley, "From Terror to Genocide," 80.
89. Norman James Brian Plomley, *Weep in Silence: A History of the Flinders Island Aboriginal Settlement with the Flinders Island Journal of George*

Augustus Robinson (Hobart: Blubber Head Press, 1987), 172. See also Lyndall Ryan, *The Aboriginal Tasmanians* (St. Leonards, New South Wales: Allen & Unwin, 1996).

90. Promley, *Weep in Silence:* 172. Sometimes survivors were sent to orphanages or other island locations. See Ryan, *The Aboriginal Tasmanians.*
91. Breen, "Extermination, Extinction, Genocide," 6.
92. James Erskine Calder, "Some Account of the Wars of Extirpation, and Habits of the Native Tribes of Tasmania," *The Journal of the Anthropological Institute of Great Britain and Ireland* 3 (1974): 7–29.
93. Ibid., 8.
94. Ibid.
95. Ibid.
96. Ibid., 9.
97. Ibid.
98. Ibid., 11.
99. Ibid.
100. Ibid., 13.
101. Ibid.
102. Ibid., 14–15.
103. Ibid., 16.
104. Ibid., 19.
105. Ibid., 21.
106. Ibid., 24.
107. James W. Agnew, "The Last of the Tasmanians," *Proceedings of the Australasian Association for the Advancement of Science* 1 (1888): 478–481.
108. Ibid., 479.
109. Ibid.
110. Ibid., 478–479.
111. Ibid., 478.
112. Ibid.
113. Crowther, "The Final Phase," 8.
114. Ibid., 8–29.
115. Ibid., 28–29.
116. Barta, "'They Appear to Vanish,'" 519–539.
117. Ibid.
118. Clive Turnbull, *Black War: The Extermination of the Tasmanian Aborigines* (Melbourne: F. W. Cheshire, 1948).
119. Ryan, *Aboriginal Tasmanians*, 255. See also Jared Diamond, "In Black and White," *Natural History* 97, no. 10 (October 1988): 8–14.
120. Barta, "Relations of Genocide," 227–232.
121. Reynolds, *Fate of a Free People*, 255.
122. Moses, "An Antipodean Genocide?" 99.

123. National Indian Child Welfare Association, *Bringing Them Home: National Inquiry into the Separation of Aboriginal and Torres Strait Islander Children from Their Families* (Sydney: Human Rights and Equal Opportunity Commission, 1997).
124. Ibid., 275.
125. See Neill Levi, "'No Sensible Comparison'?: The Place of the Holocaust in Australia's History Wars," *History & Memory* 19, no. 1 (Spring/Summer 2007): 124–156.
126. Reynolds, *An Indelible Stain?*
127. Promley, *The Aboriginal/Settler Clash.*
128. See various contributors to "Footnotes to a War," *The Sydney Morning Herald*, last modified December 13, 2003, https://www.smh.com.au/national/footnotes-to-a-war-20031213-gdhzmz.html; Rhiannon Shine, "Tasmania's Difficult History: Monuments Leave Out Dark Side to Colonial Past," *ABC News*, last modified August 30, 2017, https://www.abc.net.au/news/2017-08-31/monuments-to-tasmanias-colonial-past-have-dark-side/8851554
129. On *Quadrant* see Ben Kiernan, "Cover-Up and Denial of Genocide," *Critical Asian Studies* 34, no. 3 (June 2002): 163–92.
130. Madley, "From Terror to Genocide," 81.
131. Windschuttle, *Fabrication*, 399.
132. Keith Windschuttle, quoted in Paul Sheehan, "Our History Not to Be Rewritten by Put Right," *Sydney Morning Herald*, last modified November 24, 2002, paragraph 10, http://www.smh.com.au/articles/2002/11/24/1037697982065.html
133. See Price, "Overcoming the Myth of Extinction," 68–90.
134. Keith Windschuttle, "The Fabrication of Aboriginal History," *The Sydney Papers* 15, no. 1 (Summer, 2003): 21–29. http://www.kooriweb.org/foley/resources/pdfs/197.pdf
135. Ibid., 23.
136. Ibid., 24.
137. Ibid., 26.
138. Ibid.
139. Ibid.
140. Ibid.
141. Ibid.
142. Shayne Breen, "Extermination, Extinction, Genocide," 90.
143. Ibid., 90.
144. For a list of some of the alleged killing sites see Lyndall Ryan, "List of Multiple Killings of Aboriginals in Tasmania: 1804–1835," *Online Encyclopedia of Mass Violence*, March 5, 2008, http://www.massviolence.org/IMG/article_PDF/List-of-multiple-killings-of-Aborigines-in-Tasmania-1804.pdf

145. Henry Reynolds, "Foreword," Nicholas Clement, *The Black War: Fear, Sex and Resistance in Tasmania* (St. Lucia: University of Queensland Press, 2014).
146. McGregor, "Review: *The Black War*," 466.
147. Nicholas Clements, *The Black War: Fear, Sex and Resistance in Tasmania* (St. Lucia: University of Queensland Press, 2014).
148. McGregor, "Review: *The Black War*," 466.
149. Tom Lawson, *The Last Man: A British Genocide in Tasmania* (New York: I. B. Tauris, 2014), 127.
150. Madley, "From Terror to Genocide," 78.
151. Ibid., 81.
152. Ibid., 106.
153. Edmonds, "'Our History Is Not the Last Word,'" 152–153.
154. Ibid., 156.
155. Moses, "Genocide and Settler Society," 30.

CHAPTER 3

The Indigeneity Wars: Academic and Public Refusals to Recognize Al-Nakba

Abstract In this chapter the author notes the ways that recent events have helped raise consciousness about al-Nakba, the "catastrophe," that began in 1948 with the ouster of more than 700,000 Arab Palestinians during the 1948 Israeli War of Independence. This chapter shows that further debates are needed about al-Nakba politics because for many years few outside of ranks of the "new" Israeli historiographers were willing to contemplate the possibility that some type of ethnic cleansing had taken place during the 1948 expulsions. Using the work of writers such as Ilan Pappé and Benny Morris as touchstones, the author puts on display the varied academic, legal, political, and military reasons why so few want to include the Nakba in the traditional canons of genocidal studies.

Keywords Al-Nakba • Ethnic cleansing • Great March of Return • Israeli War of Independence • "New" Israeli historiographers

In this chapter I continue my defense of critical genocide studies and decolonization debates by interrogating some of the Israeli and Western reactions to Palestinian or other Arab claims that the Israeli ouster of Arab-Palestinian refugees during and after 1948 constituted a type of "politicide,"[1] "memoricide,"[2] "mini-holocaust,"[3] "ethnic cleansing,"[4] "spacio-cide,"[5] or "indigenocide."[6]

M. Hasian, Jr., *Debates on Colonial Genocide in the 21st Century*,
https://doi.org/10.1007/978-3-030-21278-0_3

In spite of renascent interest in Nakba studies—or maybe because of this renaissance of interest—even those who are sympathetic to the Palestinian positions find ways of using alternative terms in place of "genocide," reflecting the neo-liberal power of the Auschwitz-centered, or Lemkin-like ways, of determining what does, or does not, qualify as a genocide that deserves redress.

As I explain in more detail below, for some living in the Global North those who try to characterize the birth of Israel as some sort of "Nakba" (or "catastrophe" in Arabic), are advancing ridiculous claims.[7] However, for others who are living in the Global South twenty-first-century talk of the "Nakba" symbolizes recovery of lost histories and belated recognition of older imperial or colonial abuses that are not usually discussed in "modern" studies of the Holocaust or genocides.[8]

Although the recent "Great March of Return" in Gaza helped revive interest in this topic, al-Nakba has been a perennial issue for many Israelis and Palestinians, especially after the advent of what is called "post-Zionism" or the "New Israeli historiography." There are clear political reasons why, in 2011, the Israeli Knesset passed a law that denied state funding to any public or governmental entity that treated the Nakba as a legitimate historical event that provided an occasion for mourning.[9]

Sadly, two communities—who have each seen their own share of traumatic moments—have already engaged in heated exchanges over everything from water rights to land dispossession to the best ways to interpret the British Balfour doctrine. They also carry on transgenerational disputation as they disagree about which communities suffer the most from threats of ethnic cleansing. More than a few Israelis want to argue that they are the indigenous communities and that the Palestinians are the settlers.[10]

Scholars and readers who follow some of this disputation will find that debates about the Nakba follow some familiar story lines that look very much like other colonial settler disputation in places like Tasmania or Namibia,[11] but these generic arguments have to be adapted to suit the particular needs of those who are living in Israel or occupied Palestine. Bashir Bashir and Rachel Busbridge, writing in 2018, argued that even more "decolonization" is needed in cases like this because any referencing of colonialism in "Palestine/Israel" appears to be "an outlier to the period of decolonization," where the "Israeli state was established precisely at the moment" when "much of the world began to decolonize."[12]

This chapter argues that while most global citizens may not be familiar with some of these Nakba disputes many social media outlets will help familiarize communities with the genocidal claims that circulate during these indigeneity wars. The heterogeneous nature of this disputation and the indeterminacy of historical texts contribute to situations where more social agents in the twenty-first century are becoming involved in Nakba commemoration or denialism.

It is important that scholars and readers understand the argumentative features of these conversations because at the present time both Israelis and Palestinians use everything from oral testimony to scripture, archaeology to "Google" maps,[13] history and mythmaking, to argue about how each of these communities was the "first" to inhabit and cultivate these regions.

Israelis view the formation of Israel as an "anti-colonial" or "anti-imperial" venture, where Jewish freedom fighters threw off the yoke of British mandate rule, while Palestinians try to argue that the rise of Israel simply provided Europeans and Americans with colonial wine that filled new neo-imperial bottles.

From a critical genealogical vantage point authors and readers probably need to begin studies of these complex issues by noting that these indigeneity wars have produced all sorts of grammars, and that the waging of these rhetorical campaigns provides a variety of what Michael Rothberg has called "multi-directional" and "competitive" memories.[14] Multi-directional memories are the types of memories that can co-exist and can be used to raise consciousness about two or more catastrophic events. For example, if the US Holocaust Memorial provides a platform for helping educate audiences about the 800,000 Tutsi and Hutu lives that were lost during the Rwandan genocide then this would be an example of a constructive, "multi-directional" memory formation. However, if epistemic talk of one genocide is used to try and attack the ontological existence, or the memorialization, of another genocide, then this would reflect what Rothberg calls a "zero-sum" game situation that leads to unhealthy "competitive" memory formations.

Some scholars, politicians, and laypersons are aware of the potential existence of these multi-directional or competitive memories, and they encourage others to refrain from intervening in what they view as non-productive victimage wars. It should not be assumed that all Israelis or Palestinians, or their supporters, speak in monolithic ways. For example, Edward Said, a famous Palestinian public intellectual, once refused to "equate mass extermination with mass dispossession,"[15] even though he felt that both Israelis and Palestinians were victims of European colonial ventures. When Ehud Olmert, the former leader of the centrist Kadima party in Israel, attended an Annapolis peace conference in 2007 he referenced the suffering of those Palestinian Arabs who became refugees and were denied their right of return.[16]

Given these varied ways of configuring the 1948 war, how are today's scholars or publics supposed to respond to the growing movements in critical genocide studies and colonial settler studies that are inviting researchers and publics to rethink the ways that they have positioned not only the Holocaust, but many other large-scale massacres or atrocities that were carried out during colonial or imperial years?

As I will argue in other parts of this book, answers to those questions cannot, and should not, be found by simply deploying restrictive interpretations of physical or biological genocide that were popularized by those who built on the work of Raphael Lemkin or those who drafted the UN Convention on Genocide. It is time that we acknowledge that public deliberation, and political events, impact the ways that so many make distinctions between what happened during 1948 and the "real" genocides. It is the study of the absence or the presence of political will, and not the discovery of the best definitions of genocide, that should be key.

Definitions and usages of genocidal labels can, and should change, especially in situations where debates over colonial empires bring needed revisionism and new insights into everyday life in the colonies. However, even the discovery of the best interpretations of Lemkin's work on "cultural genocide" does little to help resolve matters when national or international communities pay scant attention to that discovery. The partial, contingent, and contradictory nature of genocidal rhetorics and international humanitarian laws means that contestation and power/discourse/knowledge formations are at the center of these Israeli-Palestinian indigeneity wars.

All invested social agents who witness these debates between Israelis and Palestinians need to acknowledge that the archival descriptions of events that may have transpired between the 1880s and 1948 are not innocent, arhetorical representations of "what happened" in prior years. All texts and visualities, regardless of their purveyors' claims regarding transparency and facticity, are constitutive in nature, oftentimes constructing the very histories and memories that become a part of these indigeneity wars.[17]

Investigative journalists and members of the public are just some of the social agents who are well aware of the ideological nature of some of the politics behind much of grammatological wrangling that takes place over how to best characterize particular historical events. At different junctures in time various Israeli diplomats, scholars, and laypersons have disagreed about whether the word "Nakba" should be used to describe what happened during what Israelis call the 1948 "War of Independence." In 2009, for example, Ian Black reported on how Israel's prime ministry had ordered the removal of the word "Nakba" from school textbooks that were designed for young Arab children.[18] This decision, made by Benjamin Netanyahu's Likud-led government, seemed to be aimed at defending traditional Zionists historical narratives that might be critiqued, or undermined, by the circulation of competing contextualizations of what happened in 1948. Netanyahu, explained Black, "spoke for many Jewish Israelis" when he argued that the use of the world "Nakba" in Arab schools was "tantamount to spreading propaganda against Israel."[19] An Arab MP in the Knesset at that time, Hana Sweid, accused the Netanyahu government of "Nakba denial."[20] The Israeli minister of education, Gideon Sarr, responded to these allegations by noting that no country in the world had any educational curriculum that allowed the referencing of the creation of "a country as a 'catastrophe.'"[21]

Critical scholars might argue that this provides a perfect example of what Michael Rothberg and others would call "competitive" memory formations, where all sorts of incommensurable and contradictory rhetorical fragments are used to produce oppositional *epistemes.* In Foucauldian terms, this is a clash between histories and counter-histories, memories and counter-memories, and these competing grids of governmentalities and intelligibilities are used to try and produce "effective histories."

Those living in Israel or in occupied Palestine or in Gaza understand the stakes involved in these debates, but few laypersons in the West seem to have heard about Al Nakba. Ilan Pappé would write in 2006 that he was perplexed by the "deep chasm" that existed between the "reality and the representation" of this conflict. He elaborated by averring that it "is difficult to understand how events perpetrated in modern times" like the Nakba, that were "witnessed by foreign reporters and U.N. observers," could be "systematically denied, not even recognized as historical fact, let alone acknowledged as a crime that needs to be confronted, politically as well as morally."[22]

What is this "Nakba" that Pappé is referencing? Is he talking about the tens of thousands of Palestinian lives that have been lost between 1948 and 2018 during struggles that others label as "wars" or "terrorism"? Is he referencing the dispossession that occurred just after 1948, or is he commenting on the incremental destruction of cultures and lifestyles that follows in the wake of never-ending settlement and expansionism? What can Pappé possibly mean when he references some major "crime"?

I will continue my critique in this chapter by providing readers with a brief explanation of how some Israeli academics may have inadvertently opened a proverbial "Pandora's Box" of arguments about colonial indigenocide or genocide in Palestine.

I will have more to say about that "Pandora's Box" in the next chapter, but for now, suffice it to say that all of this becomes even more complicated after scholars and others try to assess how any of this can be symbolically linked to wars, settlements, the building of "separation walls," incursions into Gaza, the movement of embassies, and talk of one- or two-state solutions to seemingly intractable problems.

Benny Morris, the "New Israeli Historians," and the Critiques of the Mythic and Miraculous Birth of Zionist Israel

Benny Morris—who is now viewed as a staunch defender of Zionist policies—was once considered to be one of the "post-Zionist" historiographers who were accused by many Israelis of stirring up trouble during the 1980s when they critiqued the traditional Zionist narratives of the Israeli War of Independence.[23] In a famous 1988 essay in *Tikkun* Morris argued:

> The new history is one of the signs of a maturing Israel (though no doubt, there are those who say it is a symptom of decay and degeneration). What is now being written about Israel's past seems to offer us a more balanced and more "truthful" view of that country's history .... It may also, in some obscure way. serve the purposes of peace and reconciliation between the warring tribes of that land.[24]

A dozen years later, with the advent of the Second Intifada, Morris seemed to have changed some his views regarding future prospects for peace, and there are those who contend that his conclusions evolved in ways that reflected changes in Israeli—Palestinian relationships.

Morris, intentionally, or unintentionally, would find that his arguments and his archival materials would become entangled in Nabka political disputation, and his individual views would become ciphers for more collective tensions and ideological formations.

For more than 70 years many Israeli researchers, journalists, military planners, and others have admitted that incidents like the killings of between 100 and 250 civilians at Deir Yassin in April of 1948 can be documented from materials that can be found in Israel Defense Force archives, but this is contextualized as an atypical incident that proves the rule of Jewish avoidance of civilian casualties during wartime.[25] Unlike the disorderly and barbarous Palestinian and Arab enemies, the IDF and Jewish settlers who fought to avoid being pushed "into the sea" did so by following the Geneva Convention rules.

In theory, Israelis who prize free speech can talk publicly about these wartime incidents because they do not feel that Deir Yassin has stained the honor of those civilian leaders who objected to these reprehensible acts. Acknowledging Deir Yassin thus becomes a major rhetorical strategy for those who contend that talk of Al-Nakba, and speculations about many massacres, is used and abused by Palestinians and other critics of Israelis as a way of "delegitimating" the nation of Israel. Israelis and their supporters can tell stories of the "Farhud," where the Mufti of Jerusalem and his relationship with the Nazis are said to have threatened to bring the Holocaust to Levant shores.[26] If Israeli or Zionist critics are going to talk about any Palestinian catastrophe, indigenocide, or ethnic cleansing, then Israeli supporters can rebut this by writing about the treatment of Jews in Iraq and other Arab nations during and after the 1940s.

This provides yet another example of the diverse cluster of arguments that can be used in the indigeneity wars that can be symbolically and materially linked to imperial pasts, (post)colonial presents, and nationalistic futures.

In the same way that twentieth-century generations of Holocaust and genocide researchers once debated about the importance of finding the "smoking gun" that showed that Hitler or other leading Nazis planned the Judeocide at places like the Wannsee Conference, we now have heated twenty-first-century conversations about how Ben Gurion or others knew about the wartime atrocities that took place during the "transfer" of Palestinian populations and the destruction of more than 500 villages between 1947 and 1949.[27]

Palestinian researchers, archivists, interviewers, and others who help chronicle these events now have transcontinental allies who collect oral histories that are filled with tales of the rape of women and the killing of innocent children during the involuntary transfers of the 1940s.

However, as noted above, oftentimes what one views as empirical evidence, or how one views particular historiographical methods, influences how one reacts to the conclusions that are reached about the characterization of the 1948 Israeli War of Independence. One group's "primary" evidence from collected oral histories can become another group's propaganda.

For those who privilege the written word—especially when those written words appear in Israeli military archives—these "oral" Palestinian accounts can be summarily dismissed as the Arab or Palestinian weaponized texts or "lawfare" (the political use of law) that is used to counter the "hasbara" (public diplomacy) of the Israelis.

Instead of trying to triangulate these sources and finding common ground for any constructive, imaginative multi-directional memory production contentious communities fight about the interpretative meaning of the materials on the 1940s found in the archives in the same ways they fight over separation walls, UN declarations, the legality of targeted killings, the right of return, and the legitimacy of Israeli settlements.

It is fair to say that most liberal and conservative Israeli scholars are convinced that a review of available archival materials reveals the "truth" that those in the Yishuv never had any systematic plan for the total annihilation of Palestinian villagers. Transfer, removal, and the control of the mobility of refugees who tried to return are not viewed as Zionist acts that have anything to do with cultural genocide.

Some of the "new" Israeli historians were willing to write about massacres that were committed by both sides during the 1948 fighting. Benny Morris has argued that when the Israeli archivists "opened their doors" to researchers, this provided some basic "corroboration of the Arab claim" that a "series of atrocities" had been committed at Deir Yassin.[28] However, Morris was unwilling to agree with those who generalized from this, and he went on to argue that the carrying out of multiple massacres was an inherent part of Haganah planning for Arab-Palestinian dispossession of indigenous villages. The opening of some key Israeli archives, Morris averred, "offered no corroboration of the tale of one-large scale organized massacre—by which is meant the lining up against a wall or a field or building of dozens, hundreds, or thousands of unarmed civilians and the execution of individuals."[29] Yes, there were stories of grenades being tossed into village homes, the killing of some civilians during hand-to-hand combat, and so on, but this could be chalked up to the incidental horrors suffered by those who witnessed the ravages of typical modern warfare.

From a critical genealogical vantage point, Morris' framing of the Nakba blurs the lines between the *ontological* perpetuation of those crimes and the *epistemic* representations of those deeds that were left by motivated Israelis in their own archives. He seems to be assuming that true histories can only be discovered and chronicled by those who travel to Israeli archives and those who take the time to decode Israeli military records of the 1948 events. In theory, if scholars and others cannot find archival evidence of a major massacre or any systematic Israeli plan, then that shows that some major, organized catastrophic event like the Nakba did not, and could not, have happened.

Absence of epistemic, archival materials on a historical subject can be used as positivist proof that something did not happen during the 1940s. In one typical Benny Morris essay on Deir Yassin readers will find no discussion of the traditional laws of armed conflict that protected civilians during the late 1940s, and readers will search in vain if they are looking for any detailed commentary that highlights the problems that might manifest themselves when Jewish soldiers destroyed villages or planted mines to deter Palestinians from exercising their own "right of return." In many portions of his essay Morris writes in an objectivist style that looks dispassionate and unbiased, but when he turns his attention to some of the most controversial, contentious claims that can be made about indeterminate texts his tone changes as he interjects himself into the Nakba debates. As he comments on Deir Yassin he cannot help presenting his own subjective, personal opinions on the representative nature of this massacre or the motivations of those he believed were fighting a righteous war. His essay contains his impressions regarding what does, or does not, constitute a "massacre," and he can strategically do this without any discussion of International Hague rules or Geneva Convention edicts. Instead, Morris focuses on Israeli laws, Israeli military codes, Yishuv goals, and Jewish fighters' abilities to counter the military maneuvers of British soldiers, the Arab Legion, or the Palestinian militias.

Benny Morris, in his Deir Yassin essay and his other works, crafted a discursive symbolic narrative that resonated with Israeli moderates and leftists during the 1980s and 1990s. He seemed to be critiquing the traditional histories that were told about Israeli innocence and the absence of any massacres, but he did not distance himself from liberal Zionism as his histories also recorded the supposed existential dangers that confronted those in the Yishuv. Morris' wartime framing of Deir Yassin, and his contextualization of the Israeli War of Independence, treated any abuses that took place during the transfer actions as sad but understandable incidents of modern warfare. Moreover, by focusing on specific incidents in 1948 Morris can avoid having to be the Nakba as a structure or ongoing process.

Here there is no grappling with the nuances of international humanitarian law (IHL) principles of distinction, proportionality, humanity, necessity, and so on. Knowledgeable readers, who may be familiar with the work of Ilan Pappé, might even speculate that Benny Morris, in his essays on topics like Deir Yassin, is trying to anticipate, or rebut, the charges of those who claim that all of this needs to be viewed as "ethnic cleansing."[30]

For years many conservative Israelis and Israeli supporters outside of Israel attacked Morris and lumped him together with the more radical "new" Israeli historiographers or "post-Zionists," but he redeemed himself in their eyes when his later works focused in on the existential dangers that were posed by Yishuv enemies during 1948.

Many social scientists are trained to prize and privilege the positivistic nuggets of truth that can be mined in the archives, and with the passage of years—and the rising power of Netanyahu administrations—Morris is oftentimes treated as someone that Derrideans might recognize as the embodiment of the mythic "archon," the defender of treasured archives.[31]

Given the sensitive nature of Holocaust and genocide studies for Israeli scholars, readers can understand some of the hostility of those who are infuriated when the Israeli "War of Independence" is linked to terms like "catastrophe" or "indigenocide." In many accounts of "what happened" during 1948 it is not always easy to separate out the secular from the sacred, myth from fact, or description from prescription as presentist needs influence the acceptance or rejection of interpretations of archival materials.

Is it any wonder that Benny Morris, after reviewing the work of Uri Milstein and Walid Khalidi on Deir Yassin, opined in 2005 that we needed to revise the estimates of some of the recorded dead from 1948? He averred that the "number of Arab dead was far smaller than hitherto published," and he noted that this "implicitly undermined the large-scale 'massacre' charge."[32] Morris concluded his essay on Deir Yassin by arguing:

> Combatants and noncombatants were gunned down in the course of house-to-house fighting, and subsequently after the battle groups of prisoners and noncombatants were killed in separate, sporadic acts of frenzy and revenge in different parts of the village and outside Deir Yassin. The remaining villagers were then expelled. But this was no Srebrenica.[33]

This is a fascinating way of trying to create the impression that one is critiquing state denialism while at the same time quarantining that same state from genocidal allegations.

The historiographic approach allows Morris to selectively choose when to fragment and when to bring coherence to the archival materials that he is finding. By using only Israeli sources, and by focusing on Israeli military shards of evidence in the archive, he can report back to his readers that those in the Yishuv must have sought out peaceful ways of overseeing the transfers of populations that were only occasionally marked by "sporadic acts" of revenge. Yishuv and Israeli writers who place materials in the Israeli archives are not viewed as potential perpetrators of crimes, but as bystanders or victims who are fairly describing what they are witnessing.

How, after reading this type of analysis from Morris, could any reasonable person conclude that these expulsions of Palestinians were genocidal in nature?

The way that Morris writes his monolithic, positivist history—that goes into detail about what happened at this or that battle or crossroad—is itself fragmentary and helps disaggregate much of the information that can be found in Israeli or Palestinian or other archives. When he comes across evidence from Ben Gurion or some Israeli commander talking about existential danger this is used as epistemic evidence of an uncontestable ontological fact. Those arguments about perceived existential dangers are then used in the crafting of "self-defense" types of Zionist narratives that rationalize Israeli reterritorialization of Palestine.

Why does Morris even mention Srebrenica if his essays and books are supposed to provide unvarnished, descriptive truths about what happened in 1948?

Critical scholars who are advocating for more nuanced ways of studying genocidal rhetorics would argue that this is an example of normative disputation over colonial or postcolonial histories that masquerades as dispassionate, accurate, and descriptive analysis of past historical events. As Professor Ann Stoler has recently argued, archival claims and communal mentalities can often be found in some unlikely places, and those who claim to be discovering archival materials are oftentimes social agents who are *co-producing those very discoveries.*[34] Quotidian, presentist concerns impact interpretive framings of Nakba/War of Independence histories and memories.

I have spent this time unpacking this example of a Benny Morris claim so that readers can get a textured feeling for why so many Israelis—including leftists—have a difficult time listening to arguments that come from Palestinians or other Arabs who want to talk and write about Al Nakba. One group's consciousness-raising can be interpreted as another's unnecessary traumatizing.

Is this accurate historicizing, revisionism, or denialism?

If we go back and critically unpack some of the Morris claims that circulated in his Deir Yassin essay we would find that in many ways he is not just writing about the purity of arms of the 1948 Yishuv freedom fighters, but the rectitude of *the current IDF forces* that Benny Morris sees as engaged in legitimate and necessitous "counter-terrorism." His essay on Deir Yassin is a type of representative Zionist *episteme* that contains clusters of contestable assertions. What few Israeli journalists or Western scholars have noticed are the ways that Morris uses traditional Post-Nuremberg "biological" and "physical" criteria, and not "cultural" criteria for genocides, to stave off criticism that any Israeli forces engaged in any behavior that might be deemed to be genocidal in nature. A very different conclusion would be reached by John Docker in 2017, when he argued that "cultural genocide," along "with other aspects of genocide entwine and constitute each other as part of Zionist Israeli's coordinated and convergent genocide plan to destroy and replace the Indigenous society of Historic Palestine."[35]

Morris may have realized that many of his readers would recognize that Srebrenica has become a metonym for the larger horrors that were perpetrated after the break-up of the old Yugoslavia. He must have been aware that referencing the number of Srebrenica deaths (usually listed as between 8000 and 9000)[36] as genocidal acts could be contrasted by his readers with the smaller figures of Palestinian or other Arab dead in 1948. A savvy Morris managed to find ways of countering Palestinian arguments without legitimating Nakba references.

At the same time Benny Morris may have thought that his own twenty-first-century research on alleged massacres during 1948 conflicts was providing some novel, unbiased, and apolitical corrective that looked nothing like conventional hagiographic Israeli renditions of the War of

Independence, but a genealogical review of the collective work of "new" Israeli historians shows that he was simply reassembling, in convincing ways, arguments and tropes that had been circulating for generations.

The Morris essays and books resonated with Israeli audiences because they seemed to confirm their own beliefs. They too were willing to admit that a few massacres might have taken place, but war will be war, and the IDF archives also contain evidence of atrocities that might have been committed by Israel's Arab enemies.

Moral equivalence arguments are often associated with commentary of wars, and the wartime framings that were used to characterize Palestinian liberation efforts could provide myriad ways of responding to the occasional talk of al-Nakba that appeared on discursive horizons before the 2018 Gaza March of Return.

Morris' revisionist framing of the Israeli War of Independence—especially after 2001—reflected and refracted how many Israelis want to remember "what happened" between the 1930s and the end of their War of Independence. The key for many Israelis and international Israeli supporters was not just his discussion of some potential 1948 massacres but the way that his militaristic framing could be used to highlight past and present existential dangers that demanded the use of "defensive" force.

It makes sense that critical genocide scholars and readers view all of this as parts of ongoing process of indigenous debate instead of some single event involving retrieval of unvarnished truths about "what happened" in 1948. In fascinating ways, the more that writers like Bennie Morris try to argue against the "catastrophe" thesis, the more that they contribute to the production of archival materials and interpretations that could be appropriated for cross-purposes.

Instead of accepting Morris' claims about the "sporadic" nature of incidents like Deir Yassin Palestinian scholars and leftist Israeli researchers could argue that most Israeli researchers have vastly underestimated the amount of violence that took place during the Nakba.

Critical genocide scholars, for example, could produce synthetic works that brought together the very materials that Morris tried to disaggregate. Instead of uncritically accepting some of the arguments and evidence found in *military materials* that were left for the Israeli archives, critical genocide scholars and other international researchers could highlight the revelations that came from interviews with Palestinian survivors who witnessed many atrocities before they were expelled from the Yishuv.

The more that Morris started to include in his essays materials on the Second Intifada and presentist IDF practices. the more that his critics problematized his various contextualizations of the Israeli War of Independence.[37]

Many of the "new" historiographers appreciated Morris' efforts while they disagreed with some of his politics and some of his conclusions. Until the late 1980s the conventional Zionist accounts of the Israeli "War of Independence" served as the dominant stories of "what happened" during 1948, and Avi Shlaim—another of the "new Israeli historians"—has helped demystify some of these rhetorical features of these influence *epistemes.*[38] Shlaim and other leftists argue that those in the Yishuv, who were supported by communities of Jews in America and Europe, produced morality plays that included discussions about "tohar haneshek," or purity of arms, where the Zionists who fought the War of Independence were characterized as moral warriors fighting that defensive war that I referenced earlier.

These types of arguments divided the ranks of Israeli historians and other researchers who disagreed about everything from methodological choices to the conclusions that were reached by those who talked and wrote about this or that "invented" Middle Eastern history.

While some of the "new" Israeli historians were not always sure about how they felt about some of the Nakba claims coming from Palestinian quarters they shared an interest in critiquing conventional tales that were told about 1948 conflicts. Some of these dominant narratives about the Israeli War of Independence, that Professor Shlaim contends were "not history in the proper sense,"[39] would help establish the foundational Israel myths that were co-produced by many generations of social agents.

Those who co-produced the hagiographic accounts of a redemptive Israeli War of Independence included veterans who fought in 1948, journalists, biographers, and laypersons who often described the 1948 battles as opportunities for miraculous victories. Post-Zionists averred that these nationalistic morality plays configured those in the Yishuv as Biblical characters who could play the role of David, and while members of the Arab coalition played the role of Goliath.[40]

Again, the notion that any of this had anything to do with war crimes, or the systematic destruction of indigenous communities, seemed far-fetched for those who shared these Zionist beliefs or nationalistic aspirations.

As the conventional Israeli story goes, as soon as the British announced the expiration of their Mandate in this region "seven Arab states sent their armies into Palestine with the firm intention of strangling the Jewish state at birth."[41] Although a few Israeli writers living during this period questioned these conventional tales—Gavriel Cohen, Yaacov Shimoni, Meir Pa'il, and so on—it would be David Ben Gurion's supporters and believers in the dominant Zionist *dispositif* who were able to control the shape and contours of the popular histories and the collective memories that would circulate for several decades.

Critical scholars are convinced that pro-Zionist Israeli storytellers were able to accomplish some of these national legitimation tasks by creating auras that swirled around Israeli archives. Some "new" Israel historians targeted these auras, and they tried to create fissures and ruptures in these traditional Zionist *epistemes.*

Benny Morris' 2005 story about Deir Yassin shows us some of the ways that the leftist interpretations of some of the "new" post-Zionist positions could be refuted, and his twenty-first-century essays provided one more echo chamber for those who already believed in the veracity of the traditional IDF interpretations of "war" horrors and in the Israeli purity of arms narratives.

Some members of the Israeli public were enamored with the intriguing arguments of many post-Zionists, but both the violence of the Second Intifada as well as the rise of Netanyahu provided signals that the Israeli moderates were moving toward the right and were joining those who now wanted to legitimate settlements in places that were now called "Judea" and "Samaria." This (re)appropriation of ancient Biblical names also served to answer the claims of international Israeli critics who continued to call the West Bank and East Jerusalem "occupied Palestinian" territories.

During the first few decades of the twenty-first century many Israelis not only returned to hagiographic studies of the 1948 War but linked them to acts such as the IDF incursions into Gaza. Now younger generations of Israelis were once again hearing the heroic Israeli tales that would be told about what happened during the Israeli War of Independence, with their stereotypical antagonists and protagonists. The defensive and exclusionary nature of the mass-mediated circulation of these tales leaves very little cultural, historical, or political space for any multi-directional stories of the victims, those who died, or those who were dispossessed. Elderly Palestinians can be configured as UN "refugees" who politicize Al Nakba and (mis)remember the Israeli War of Independence.

In part, this is because the revitalized hegemonic Zionist tales that are told about the 1948 War of Independence configure those in the Yishuv as the victims of all sorts of perfidy. For example, it might be the treachery that was coming from the Arab countries during the Farhud. Alternatively, the focus could be on the acts of the deceptive British imperialists who used their "White Paper" to try and prevent Israeli migration during the European Holocaust. It was said that Jews living in the Yishuv had to overcome a variety of political or military obstacles that were placed in their paths by British imperialists or King Abdullah in Transjordan and his breaking of bilateral agreements.

Regardless of the chosen permutations of these arguments these Israeli stories had few characters in them who had anything to do with any Palestinian "catastrophe."

To be fair to Israelis there have been times when it seemed as if vocal minorities of Israelis were at least willing to openly debate about the Nakba, but when those views started to seem threatening to Zionist aspirations substantive debate about any potential ethnic cleansing during 1948 was closed off. Censorship became another tool for those who wished to stifle talk of any Nakba.

At times these overreactions manifest themselves in ways that garner international media attention. Some journalists, for example, have noted that this is such a sensitive topic that the circulation of published research on the destruction of Palestinian coastal villages—like Teddy Katz's thesis research on Tantura—can lead to situations where authors wind up in front of judges. Legal proceedings having to do with this research have been filed after aggrieved parties complain that some researchers are collecting materials from witnesses who might have impugned the reputation of members of Jewish forces like the Alexandroni brigade who cleared some of those coastal towns.[42]

Any telling of "Al Nakba" that would have challenged what Avi Shlaim calls the "immaculate conception" telling of 1948 activities elicits immediate Israeli rebuttal. For example, writers like Shabtai Teveth attacked the group of "new" Israel historiographers who were said to be trying to charge Israel with "original sin."[43]

Several Palestinian scholars who build on the work of the "post-Zionist" Israeli scholars have pointed out that at least since 1949 there have been Arab authors who tried, with little success, to circulate nationalistic or Pan-Arab readings of the 1948 catastrophe. Few in the West paid any attention to these exact same arguments before these very same ideas and arguments were picked up and deployed by the new Israeli historians.

In other words, for any of this to be taken seriously, any talk or written commentary about al-Nakba needed to come from Israelis who debated among themselves, and only then could Palestinians gain access to the mediated outlets and venues that they needed as they produced their own "effective histories" (Foucault).

When many of these dissident framings of the Israeli War of Independence were initially presented by the new Israeli scholars they were either ignored or they were trivialized. However, over time, small, but vocal, groups of interdisciplinary academics started to talk about the contributions of the post-Zionists as they included their work in the neo-Marxist, postmodern, post-structural, or postcolonial studies of what happened between 1947 and 1949.

None of this was taking place in a vacuum. Outside of academic hallways, many who witnessed the arrival of the First Intifada (1987) and the Second Intifada (2000–2005) hoped that international interventionism, or the enforcement of UN resolutions, or renewed peace talks, might bring about two-state or one-state solutions to Palestinian-Israeli disputation.

In Israel the rising power of Netanyahu and his Israeli coalitions came at a time when Americans were coping with their own post-9/11 counter-insurgency efforts in places like Afghanistan and Iraq, and these changes influenced paradigmatic changes in the academy as well. Talk of peaceful solutions to problems in the "occupied Palestinian territories" (OPT) could now be counted with militaristic framings that prioritized the need for counter-terrorist walls, guarded roads, checkpoints, and settlers in Judea and Samaria.

As I explain in more detail below, as soon as hope for that reconciliation seemed to vanish after Oslo, the Morris position seemed to mysteriously change. This also impacted the reactions to his work.

If we go back and compare what Morris had to say in 1988 with what he wrote in 2005 the tone that he adopted changed. In that 1988 *Tikkun* essay Benny Morris once argued that "Jewish atrocities" were "far more widespread than the old historians" had indicated, and he went on to mention the massacres of Arabs at places like Al-Dawayima, Eilaboun, Jish, Safsaf, Hule, Saliha, Sasa, and Lydda. Morris explained that the "drive to avenge past Arab wrongs also contributed to the exodus."[44]

Yet mentioning possible forgotten "massacres" does not automatically mean that the new Israeli historiographers were going to pave the way for twenty-first-century talk of the indigenocide or the ethnic cleansing of the Palestinians during Al Nakba. The new historians apparently viewed themselves as purveyors of "parrhesia," battlers who risked much as they spoke in front of the powerful.[45] However, there were limits to what even post-Zionists were willing to argue as they revisited the archives. Avi Shlaim, for example, writing in 1995, acknowledged that perhaps the received historical wisdom of nation-states was in some "sense" "propaganda of the victors," and yet he, like Benny Morris, seemed to view his own research as an apolitical, objective antidote to the politicized myths that could be found in the "old" Israeli histories.[46]

While some of the new Israeli historiographies felt that they were helping peace processes by correcting historical records during the 1980s, from a critical vantage point it could be argued that it would be a mistake to forget that many Palestinians had their own views regarding the "catastrophe." Two decades after the rise of the post-Zionist historiographers Anaheed Al-Hardan argued that the material and symbolic realities of the series of wars that were fought between Israelis and Palestinians (or between the Israelis and other Arabs) had influenced the ways that we assess what she called the "transformation" of the "concept" of Al Nakba. As she explained, this particular "catastrophe" was no longer being remembered by Palestinians as the shortcomings of the "Pan-Arab" coalition members who attacked the Yishuv in 1948. Instead, in the wake of the two intifadas Al Nakba today has come to "exclusively signify the catastrophe of the Palestinian people" as an "ongoing" struggle that appears to be without resolution.[47]

Reviews of essays that appeared in Palestinian newspaper outlets such as *Al Quds* [Jerusalem] and *Al-Hayat al-Jadida* [the new life] provide support for Professor Al-Hardan's claims, and they illustrate how many Palestinians and their readers now viewed Al Nakba as a "metaphor" for their own daily suffering and for transgenerational catastrophes.[48]

Al-Hardan, in her critique, alluded to one of the most controversial aspects of Palestinian argumentation, that touched on the claim that al-Nakba was an ongoing process—a structure not an event (Patrick Wolfe)[49]—that involved the deaths or the traumatizing of generations of Palestinians after 1948. Al-Hardan elaborated by noting that Palestinians around the world had to continue to watch the building of even more Israeli settlements as well as the "indiscriminate fifty-one day slaughter in

Gaza in July 2014" [called Operation Protective Edge by the Israelis].[50] Other researchers have noted how Palestinian newspapers that were written between 1995 and 2017 commented on how Israelis tried to use censorship in the West Bank or East Jerusalem to "thwart" their Nakba commemorative performances, and they commented on the need to "undo" some of the effects of the Nakba by establishing a Palestinian state with East Jerusalem as the capital.[51]

Readers by now might be asking: What evidence can be presented that provides any indication of the lingering influence of colonial or imperial thinking on twenty-first-century Israeli decision-making or contemporary Israeli—Palestinian relations? Did the generations who lived during the 1940s and 1950s view Al Nakba as some sort of colonial genocide, or did the discussion of "ethnic cleansing" only *appear on discursive horizons in the aftermath* of the First Intifada, after 1987? After all, if so many Palestinians felt that Al Nakba was such an important part of their histories, their identities, or their collective memories, then why were so few books and articles written about these affairs before journalistic and academic coverage of the "new" Israel historians? Were melancholy Palestinians, who now saw their hopes for either a one-state solution or a two-state solution dashed, promoting revisionist histories that linked the 1947–1949 events with their witnessing of the unstoppable building of the "separation" wall, the "redemption" of "Judea" and "Samaria," and the loss of more of East Jerusalem, and so on? Was all of this helping instrumentalize Al Nakba?

Obviously these worries about the instrumentalization of a potential indigenocide, or the strategic usage of some academic discussions of an ethnic cleansing, were not new. In the same way that other participants in disputes over Tasmanian massacres, King Léopold II's Congolese practices, or Italian treatment of Ethiopians were said to be influenced by post-Holocaust epistemologies or presentist political concerns, those who now work on consciousness-raising about Al-Nakba have been accused of confusing objective "history" with public "rhetoric."

Some might respond to these claims by noting that the very "birth" of Israel depended on British recolonizing efforts. The British, one could argue, tried to make promises to *both Jews in the Yishuv and Arabs in Transjordan* in order to help maintain British imperial spheres of influence.

However, there would be those like Benny Morris who would write that it was the "prewar basic structural weaknesses of Palestinian society" that "led to the dissolution of that society when the test of battle came."[52]

Note how this not-so-veiled critique of the existence of Palestinian consciousness before war time can be used by other commentators who want to argue that all forms of Palestinian nationalism would be "invented."[53]

In spite of research conducted by Palestinians and other researchers who questioned some of the Ben-Gurion type of mythological remembrances of the Israeli War of Independence, there were relatively few transatlantic public interrogations by professional scholars of the conventional Israeli contextualizations of the War of Independence in the West. This perhaps helps explain some of the massive backlash that took place when the "new Israeli" historiographers—Simha Flapan,[54] Benny Morris,[55] Ilan Pappé,[56]and Avi Shlaim[57]—arrived on the scene during the 1980s.[58]

While most of these new Israeli historiographies, or post-Zionists made it clear that they were not trying to critique all forms of Zionism, they were attacked by other Israelis or Israeli supporters who claimed that the new historiographers were trying to help the Palestinians rationalize their indigenous search for an independent Palestinian nation.

For the most part the new Israeli historians tried to counter these accusations by appearing to avoid becoming entangled in messy, normative debates about the symbolic links that could be made between what happened in 1948 and post-1987 diplomatic concerns. Using either modernist, or mild postmodernist approaches, the new Israeli historians tried to create impression that they were merely concerned about accurate historicizing as they combed through the archives. For example, Benny Morris questioned the traditional tales that had been told about how hundreds of thousands of Palestinians simply fled their homes, without coercion from the IDF, while Ilan Pappé underscored the role that the British had played in trying to restrain some Arab neighbors in 1948. Avi Shlaim built on some of Pappé's work by elaborating on some of the reasons why "collusion" had taken place between King Abdullah of Transjordan and the Zionist movement as they both tried to counter the supposed power of the Mufti of Jerusalem.

Yet only Pappé and some of his followers talked openly about "ethnic cleansing," and this was one of the topics that became a wedge issue that divided the ranks of the new Israeli historiographers. This was, and remains, a taboo argument that is considered to be beyond the pale of "objective" academic scholarship in many circles.

For a time—especially in the decade after 1988—some hoped that the excitement generated by the buzz around the new Israeli historiographers might help open the door for Palestinian authors and other Arabs who wanted harsher critiques of 1948 affairs, but there was no shortage of those who viewed the "new" Israeli historians as political interlopers who intentionally or intentionally were hurting the State of Israel. Mordechai Bar-On argued that Ilan Pappé, in *The Ethnic Cleansing of Palestine*, was not looking "for the truth, as a historian should at least attempt to do, but rather" was volunteering his "pen to the propaganda efforts of the more extreme Palestinian elements in an attempt to delegitimate Israel and Zionism."[59]

To his credit Bar-On was willing to admit that Israelis needed to recognize the terrible price that the Palestinians "paid for the Jewish endeavor in Palestine," but he wanted Palestinians to reciprocate by taking ownership of their own social agency and admit that part of the reason why the Israeli leadership was "glad to see the Palestinians vacate a large part of the country" had to do with the ruthlessness of the 1948 war. At the same time, Bar-On wanted the Palestinians to recognize that their demand to return their "refugees to their lands and homes amounts today to a battle cry, not a plan for peace."[60] This reviewer then shows how Pappé does not "mention" the "cruel attack of Arab fighters against the convoy bringing medical and academic personnel to Mount Scopus" and how some "70 Jewish civilians died from gunfire and bombs originating from those same houses which were blown up in case of an Israeli retreat."[61]

This was some of the moral equivalence that I mentioned above.

Like other cases of alleged colonial massacres, disputes about atrocious behavior during 1948 could morph into competing, and contestable, victimage wars that had everything to do with presentist disputation.

The new Israeli historiographers were collectively critiquing not only the abuses that were carried out by the Irgun or Stern military forces but the decisions and the actions of the more centrist Haganah. Sometimes these new historiographers were also critiquing the decisions of the Jewish Agency, the National Command, the General Staff (*Ha-Mateh haklali*), and members of the Mapai party. These were some of the very communities who self-identified as preservers of their notion of purity of arms by chastising those who carried out the Deir Yassin massacre.

Imagine the consternation of those who participated in the War of Independence as they were now being asked to accept the findings of the new Israeli historians, or those who followed them and brought postcolonial studies, settler studies, genocide studies, or similar frameworks to the table. During the 1980s and 1990s writers like Avi Shlaim were magnifying the social agency of the British, who were said to have been interested in witnessing the partitioning of Palestine in ways that allowed for *both* the formation of the state of Israel as well as the implementation of the "Greater Transjordan" solution to the Palestinian problem.[62] The British, in other words, produced some novel contextualizations of 1948 events, and they were soliciting support for particular UN resolutions as a way of preserving waning British diplomatic power. This focus on the British could be used to treat those in the Yishuv as mere puppets or weaker powers.

The Advent of the Second Intifada, Reversals, and the Evolutionary Nature of 1948 Remembrances

While Simha Flapan, Benny Morris, Ilan Pappé, Avi Shlaim, and their followers have often been given credit for bringing needed correctives that revised at least some Israeli textbooks, readers need to realize that the older narrations of the War of Independence still resonated with many Jewish communities in Israel, the US, the UK, and elsewhere. While the post-Zionist "new" historians tended to configure Ben Gurion's soldiers as fighters who were protected by the UN and British bystanders, the purveyors of more patriotic traditional tales focused primarily on the heroism of the Jews in the Yishuv.

The post-Zionists used *realpolitik* arguments to study Ben-Gurion's strategizing and his use of deception, while the authors of conventional Israeli histories treated him as the leader who managed to outwit countless Arab foes.

While a few of these post-Zionists contemplated the possibility that perhaps the Israeli War of Independence could be viewed through postcolonial lens, most preferred to focus on the insights that came from objectivist and modernist studies of intellectual, military, or diplomatic histories. The usage of orthodox research methods did not prevent the new Israeli historians from viewing themselves as radicals. One of them could write in 1995 that the "debate between the old and the new historians is bitter and acrimonious," and that it was "melancholy" to have to add that there was "no sign yet of the emergence of a postrevisionist synthesis."[63]

After a decade of theorizing and arguing postcolonial critics and other critical scholars who watched these Israeli debates asked whether anyone could document how the "new" Israeli historians and their revisionism *had empirically* impacted the ways that Israeli and foreign scholars were supposed to write and talk about occupied territories, ethnical cleansing, or remembrances of Al-Nakba. The work of Avi Shlaim, for example, could be used *to moderately revise* the ways that future disputants argued about the supposed "voluntariness" of the flight of more than 750,000 Palestinian Arabs during 1948, but this could be acknowledged without necessarily accepting the more pointed claims of those who demanded that this be characterized as a major "catastrophe," indigenocide, or "genocide."

Moreover, after the advent of the First and Second Intifadas many of the so-called post-Zionists followed the lead of Benny Morris and joined their more conservative Zionist brothers and sisters. They stayed silent or refused to contextualize the Israeli War of Independence as another colonial genocide or a glaring example of frontier settler "ethnic cleansing."

By the end of the twentieth century it became apparent that how one wished to remember Al-Nakba, or the Israeli War of Independence, impacted how one argued about the legality and morality of territorial dispossession in the West Bank, the right of return for both Israelis and Palestinians, expansion of settlements, the status of East Jerusalem, the treatment of Gaza, and one or two-state solutions.

In an interesting illustration of how current events, military affairs, and diplomatic maneuverings can influence the shifting trajectories of the rhetorical histories of particular conflicts, note the ways that the advent of the Second Intifada, in 2000, impacted the remembering and forgetting of the Israeli War of Independence. The Israeli elites and members of the public who once flirted with the idea of making substantive revisions in Israeli histories, textbooks, movies, films, and so on that would be based on the findings of the "new" Israeli historians, reversed course as the IDF militarized and securitized the battles over territorial dispossession on the West Bank and Gaza.

The military, diplomatic, and religious arguments that were once used by the Palmah generation were revived and used to counter the claims of those who followed the new Israeli historians. Patriotic Israelis resented the ways that Palestinian minorities in Israel tried to treat Independence Day as a day of mourning, and a backlash could be felt as remembrances of al-Nakba were viewed as nefarious attempts at historical revisionism.

Even some of those who once characterized as members of new Israeli historian community were disenchanted with Palestinian "terrorism" and the failure to take advantage of post-Oslo extensions of the olive branch in the name of peace and security. Benny Morris argued in one of the new editions of his book, *The Birth of the Palestinian Refugee Problem* (2004), that the "atrocities" that were committed by the Haganah and other Yishuv warriors were "limited in size, scope and time."[64] This helped domesticate or qualify some of his earlier claims.

As noted above, Morris, who still relies almost exclusively on Israeli archival sources, is often reluctant to consider the possibility that there was any central, systematic, planning that would have provided any indication of intentional genocidal practices. Contrast that with Saleh Abdel Jawad's claim that between December of 1947 and January of 1949 research teams who interviewed survivors and witnesses could document that "nearly 70 massacres" had been committed, and he was adamant that this was a conservative count of these types of incidents.[65]

Would this type of claim resonate with twenty-first-century audiences?

Al-Nakba Revisionism or Post-Revisionism During the Twenty-First Century

Obviously historical and contemporary events have also influenced Palestinian as well as Israeli contextualizations of what happened during 1948. Ahmad Sa'di has argued that the histories of Nakba, like many other chronicling of events are "made of up of fragmentary and occasionally contradictory events," that are brought together by investigations into "intersubjective phenomena."[66] Professor Sa'di is in the academic camp that does not mind labeling the transfer of Palestinians in 1948 a form of "ethnic cleansing" by "Jewish settlers who had arrived from Europe almost a decade or two earlier."[67] He explained that after "Al-Nakba the Palestinians have remained in a non-communicative mood," and that this was reflected in the "dearth of published scholarly material on Al-Nakba."[68] Contemporary generations of Palestinian scholars were supposed to fill this void by collecting oral histories, visiting diverse archives, and using frames of reference that were ignored by conventional chronicles of the Israeli War of Independence.

Many Palestinians who write about the massacres that took place during Al-Nakba remind readers that during the last two decades writers like Kamal Abdul Fattah, Issa Khalaf, Beshara Doumani, and Rashid Khalidi have been busy producing general historical studies of Palestine.[69] Saleh Jawad explains that many of these writers extended the work of Arif al-Arif and Muhammad Nimr Khatif, and most rejected the "Israeli allegations that Arab leaders ordered Palestinians to evacuate their villages." Jawad admitted that this "myth" of ordered evacuation was still circulating in the popular discourse of some Arab communities, but he explained that this was because at one time Palestinian refugees had been listening to Israeli-sponsored radio messages that were used to "wage psychological warfare."[70] Jawad, who was aware of the existence of conflicting Al-Nakba memories in elite and vernacular Arab communities, nevertheless hoped that the current usage of oral histories could now be used to "bring more and more massacres to light," and that their occurrence could be "confirmed by Israeli army documents."[71]

It would be the Palestinian scholars' critiques of the new Israeli historians, as well as their adamant arguments about "ethnic cleansing," that bothered several Israeli scholars and journalists. Anita Shapira, for example, was convinced that select remembrances of the Holocaust were confounding the efforts of some who were trying to "draw simple analogies between the situation in Palestine and other colonization countries."[72] She understood that some researchers who were following the "post-Zionists" were trying to analyze "Israel as a society of immigrants-settlers in the context of colonialism," but she argued that comparisons with colonization in North America, Australia, or the "Russian colonialization of Central Asia" were sometimes used for the stigmatization of Zionism.[73]

These types of critiques—from well-respected Israeli scholars—served to underscore the point that comparative studies of colonial genocides are still volatile subjects, especially given the fact that for many Palestinians Al-Nakba was not some "war" with finite beginning and end dates, but rather the ushering in of incremental dispossession and the delegitimation of Palestinian state efforts. Is it possible that some of those who critique the Palmah generation need to include rhetorical texts that belong to what Anaheed Al-Hardan has recently called the "post-1948 Arab universe of discourse"?[74]

As Anaheed Al-Hardan explained, outside interest in studying the Nakba has waxed and waned, and researchers who approach this subject need to make sure that they listen to her admonition that they do not conflate this "discursive reading" of evolutionary transformations of the meaning of al-Nakba with "Palestinians' memories of narratives on 1948."[75] As she rightly points out, a catastrophe that was responsible for the "wholesale destruction of societies and communities, as was the case for the major part of Palestinian society in 1948," cannot be said to simply "'appear' and 'disappear' for its survivors and their descendants."[76]

In other words, we should not make the mistake of those who confuse epistemic histories with ontological realities and treat historical events as merely sophistic, negotiable materials.

Sadly, it seems to be the case that although writers like Constantine Zurayk, Musa Al-Alami, Muhammad Nimr al-Khatib, Arif al-Arif, and other Arabs had been writing about al-Nakba since 1948, Westerners did not really pay much attention to this discourse before the popularization of the work of the new Israeli historians who were credited with revising and critiquing traditional narrations of what happened during 1948. By reviving interest in these early works Palestinian scholars and activists hope to document the existence of ethnic cleansing or indigenocide at the same time that their efforts allow former victims to have their say about topics like the refugee crisis and the Palestinian right of return.

Although many Palestinian scholars or other Arab researchers are willing to admit that Jews in the Yishuv who tried to expel Palestinian-Arabs from Haifa and other parts of Palestine during the Israeli War of Independence were not always evidencing genocidal mentalities, there are no shortage of commentators who are convinced that notions of "transfer" were used for the illegal and harmful expulsion of indigenous communities in the region.[77] Joseph Massad, for example, writing in *Boundary 2*, argued that the Zionist activities in 1948 involved an attempt to "obliterate the [Arab] Palestinian landscape in an attempt to erase the traces of the Palestinians and reveal the phantasm of ancient Jewish traces."[78] Under the cover of anti-colonial warfare against the British and self-defense actions against the Arabs those in the Yishuv who wished to seize as much land as possible before UN intercession did their best to make sure that any *de jure* recognition of Israeli rights followed in the wake of de facto control of as much land as possible in these contested regions.

Many of these Arab writers acknowledged the debt that they owed Benny Morris, Ilan Pappé, and the other new Israel historians or critical sociologists. Professor Nur Masalha averred that the new historians were a part of "post-Zionist" efforts that helped with the critiquing the traditional stories of "voluntary" Arab Palestinian flight. These revisionist historiographies had forced many Israeli elites and publics to at least confront the fact that some Israelis were willing to argue that systemic violence led to the deaths of thousands of Palestinian civilians. However, Masalha complained that with the passage of years even the "new" Israeli historians ended up justifying "old and neo-colonialist ideas on 'transfer' and ethnic cleansing" that contributed to the formation of twenty-first-century discourses that threated the "Palestinians with another Nakba."[79]

Nadera Shalhoub-Kevorkian, a law professor at Hebrew University in Jerusalem, seemed to echo some of this when she argued that Zionist legal historiographies, and select remembrances of what happened in 1948, are still being used to erase Palestinian history and reject the right to mourn in ways that lead to both physical and psychological damage.[80] Walid Khalidi, who wrote some of the first Palestinian summaries of what happened during the fall of Haifa in 1959, has recently revisited these issues and concluded that the British colluded with the Haganah in ways that made sure that the use of "psychological warfare tactics" would be used in ruthless ways so that the Plan Dalet could be carried out against unarmed civilians who needed to moved out of these lands. Khalidi's 1959 writings, as well as his revised commentaries, are filled with statements about how mortars, barrels filled with car tires, and other "infernal machines" were used to wage war against hundreds of thousands of Palestinian Arabs.[81] Obviously these types of critiques look nothing like the heroic tales of battles between combatants that were circulated by defenders of the Palmah generation.

Some writers who were willing to write about "ethnic cleansing" or potential genocidal acts were also concerned about how to characterize the public and academic debates about these issues. Haifa Rashed, Damien Short, and John Docker, for example, perhaps spoke for many intellectuals who living in Gaza, the West Bank, and the Palestinian diaspora when they argued that the "Nakba Memoricide" that was waged by conventional Zionist supporters was simply a part of the "on-going process" that signified how Al-Nakba was "not merely a historic event."[82]

While writers like Anita Shapira complained about how post-Zionists were treating "history as a chronicle of injustice and misery,"[83] many Palestinian and other Arab writers are willing to compare Al-Nakba with other historical or contemporary colonial genocides. Is it possible that in the same way that international academics, journalists, legal experts, and many others have revisited the Tasmanian genocide, the Armenian genocide, what happened in South West German Africa, and so on we need to re-investigate what happened during the 1948 exodus of more than 700,000 Palestinian Arabs who either fled, or where coercively expelled, from what is now called Israel?[84]

For many Palestinians and other Arabs the recent incursions into Gaza, and all of the talk of a "third Intifada" put on display once again the urgent need to reexamine multiple facets of the Palestinian catastrophe.[85] One major issue, of course, is whether this can be done in a way that allows for multi-directional formation or whether al-Nakba memorializa-tion inherently produces competitive memories.

Readers by now can readily imagine that some of these comparative gestures have infuriated those who believe that the Israeli War of Independence has nothing to do with any talk of genocide or indigeno-cide. As Martin Shaw explained in a 2010 essay in *Holy Land Studies*, many of the scholars who study the Holocaust or other genocides "have not generally framed the question of Israel and Palestine" from "within the perspective of genocide."[86] Omer Bartov, a critic of these types of moves, has averred that if we keep stretching the definition of genocide to include topics like the Al-Nakba, then the conceptual utility of term "genocide" would unravel and lose its conceptual coherence. During a debate that took place between Martin Shaw and Bartov that appeared in the *Journal of Genocide Research* Bartov opined that if researchers kept broadening the meaning of some these terms then after saying that the Nazis practiced genocide on the Jews and Poles we would have to say that the Soviets practiced genocide on the Poles, and the Poles did the same to the Ukrainians, and so on.[87] Bartov tried to provide concrete examples to back up his assertions by noting:

> The implications of such a definition [of genocide] is that it empties the term not only of historical meaning, making it too general to be useful, but also of judicial implications. This has a bearing on the Israel-Palestinian conflict. Since there is no debate about returning Germans to Eastern Europe, Poles to Ukraine, Ukrainians to Poland, Jews to Lithuania, etc., despite their having been, by your [Shaw's] definition, victims (though often also perpetrators) of genocide, why can Palestinians claim a right of return? What makes their Naqba "better" than all others? If Germans from the Volga and the Sudetenland settled down in Freiburg, why could Palestinians not settle down in Damascus?[88]

Bartov explained that he was not "advocating" that Palestinians settle down in Damascus, but was merely trying to show Shaw the directional "logic" of his own arguments.

If this type of academic debate had stayed at some high level of abstraction—that used some variant of Raphael Lemkin's work to try to narrow or broaden the application of the word "genocide"—then this could have been characterized as a fairly tame form of scholarly disputation. It might have had little to do with the affective feelings, national identities, historiographic positions, or memories of those who participated in these debates. Yet a review of the lengthy "discussion" that took place between Shaw and Bartov reveals how these scholarly disputes often drift into presentist, ideological academic, or public argumentation.

The Shaw-Bartov scholarly debate did more than provide just hints of how international publics might react when they heard this type of disputation. Shaw quoted materials that allegedly showed the continued presence of Zionist, "incipient genocidal mentality" toward Arab societies, settler-colonial genocide, and exclusionary Israeli nationalism,[89] while Bartov responded by contending that Shaw was forgetting that Jews in 1948 were facing massive existential dangers. Bartov argued that he was willing to acknowledge that Israel needed to come to terms with the flight of some 750,000 Palestinians during the War of Independence, but he would not concede that any of this violence had anything to do with genocidal intentions or practices. This was how Bartov wanted to contextualize matters:

> [C]alling 1948 a genocide is neither historically justifiable nor politically useful. The 800,000 Jews living in Palestine in 1948 were in fact faced with an existential threat—greater than that faced by Britain in 1940 and following a national catastrophe on a scale not experienced by Britain since 1066. The British killed far more German civilians in terror bombing of the cities and condoned the expulsion of 11–13 million Germans in the aftermath of the war, yet I do not see any discussion by British scholars of Britain having perpetrated genocide.[90]

Convinced that Shaw, a British researcher, was unfairly characterizing the Israeli War of Independence Bartov took the position that in the same way that it would be a "false argument" to accuse the British of genocide it would also be problematic to claim that the Jews in the Yishuv had perpetrated genocide. The "attempt to describe the establishment of the State of Israel as founded in genocide," Bartov intoned, had little to do with "historical evidence or argumentation" but instead, had something to do with an "urge to delegitimize the very existence of that state."[91]

What Bartov failed to mention is that his own scholarship and his own arguments were themselves ideological markers that represented interventions in these academic and public debates about whether or not settler colonial wartime acts could be viewed as genocidal. Whether he admitted it or not, he was using permutations from some old *epistemes* that were once used by those who attempted to legitimate Zionist expansionism and Israeli stances. Like many Israeli supporters, Bartov took Israeli's threatened survival in 1948 as an indisputable fact, and not an opinion.

I have gone into detail outlining the Shaw-Bartov dispute because it has become symptomatic of the academic and ideological nature of elite and vernacular Nakba remembrance. As a critical scholar it is not my intention to hold up some essentialized representation about what happened during the Israeli War of Independence and then claim that the other side in this argumentation is circulating falsehoods and propaganda. Nor, as I noted in other parts of this book, am I interested in trying to find "the" largest genocide or Holocaust. Instead, what I want to argue is that the use of broader conceptualizations of indigenocide—that include actions and consequences as well as intentions—should help future generations raise awareness about Al-Nakba argumentation.

Conclusion

Whether we like it or not the rhetorical histories and the public memories that we have about the Israeli War of Independence, or what Arab Palestinians call al-Nakba, are inextricably tied to competing nationalist mythologies, contested theological and political claims, and complex presentist needs. On the one hand, as countless numbers of Israelis have argued, if we talk seriously about a UN-recognized "right of return" for all of the Palestinians in refugee camps and in the diaspora then this would itself be viewed by empowered Israeli supporters as a form of delegitimation that would signal an attack on the legality of an Israeli state dominated by Zionist Jews.

On the other hand, to pretend that the Irgun, the Haganah, and the other Yishuv fighting forces only used gentle means of persuasion to get 750,000 to leave Haifa and many other Palestinian regions in 1948 can also be considered to be a form of revisionism or denialism. To argue that Palestinians voluntarily left on their own accord is itself a form of self-serving Zionist revisionism that rationalizes the growth of "returning" settlements and the continued repossession of what many Israelis or diasporic Jews regard as the God-given lands of "Judea" and "Samaria"

Give the emotional, material, and symbolic capital that has been invested by so many in these debates about Al-Nakba, it could be argued that as long as these competing nationalist tales are being crafted by various supporters of Arab-Palestinian and Israeli causes—and as long as they are viewed as mutually exclusive and contradictory—then cosmopolitan readers and other bystanders are being presented with multiple definitions of indigenocide.

In order to break this type of impasse I want to conclude by arguing that scholars can profit from the use of what Anaheed Al-Hardan has called "decolonizing research on Palestinians" that uses "critical epistemologies and research practices."[92] I would agree with her claims that some of the academic treatments of Al-Nakba that have circulated since 1948 have operated "part and parcel of the historical and contemporary colonizing power/knowledge nexus" that has tried to "block" the legitimacy of calls for any Arab-Palestinian "right of return."[93] I also agree with her claims regarding some of the reasons why the "new" Israeli historians gained the academic spotlight as some marginalized the voices of Arab-Palestinians who left us oral histories that look nothing like the materials that are stored in Israeli military archives.

Anaheed Al-Hardan's own extensions of Donna Haraway's work on "diffraction" patterns of epistemic knowledge about the Nakba need to be viewed as interventionist practices that have their own presentist aims. For example, her interviews with those who survived the Tantura village massacre or her qualitative research on how this was just one of "approximately 70 documented massacres perpetuated by Zionist militias and the incipient Israeli army"[94] are motivated, partial, contingent, and contested interpretations of Nakba historiography. Those of us who extend the work of post-structural, postmodern, or postcolonial scholars need to admit our own subject positions and the ideological nature of our academic critiques of the empowered. This, however, does not mean that we ignore the material realities of what happened during 1948, nor does it mean that we refuse to listen to Palestinian survivors' stories because of their politicized nature.

Pointing out the ideological nature of this instrumentalization does not mean that all histories or mythologies are alike, or that audiences should throw up their hands and be dismissive of all attempts at Al-Nakba consciousness-raising. Nadera Shalhoub-Kevorkian argues that the "Nakba holds multiple meanings for Palestinians" and is both a "historical event" as well as an apt description of "a larger, ongoing settler colonial structure" that "continues" to "mark the everyday" lives of Palestinians inside Israel, the territories, and the diaspora.[95]

Yet if this is the case, then we need to also understand Israeli anxieties, their worries about the adverse impact on their lives that might come from

Nakba remembrance, and the protean nature of all of this renascent elite and public interest in revisiting "what happened" during 1948. For example, if Palestinians are going to talk about potential "ethnic cleansing" or "indigenocides," then we need to admit that some Yishuv communities outside of Jerusalem may have been massacred during the early months of 1948. We can deploy impassioned critiques without necessarily claiming that we are using essentializing, objectivist frameworks for comparative genocidal analyses.

Those Palestinians who scramble to collect oral histories and testimonials before the passing of Al-Nakba generations will still have to face the fact that other chronicles have better access to extant documentary archives. Yet those of us who revisit these pasts need to think "outside the box" as we strive to investigate some of these colonial memories.

Ariella Azoulay has garnered an international reputation for her work on visual imagery and the use of pictorial depictions for the purposes of social activism. In 2009, during a gallery talk that was given at Zochrot's Tel Aviv headquarters, Azoulay analyzed some 200 photographs of the 1948 war as she explained how the Nakba was viewed by Palestinian Arabs as a disaster that was linked to production of an "Israeli regime" that hurt both Palestinians and Jewish-Israelis.[96] Visualities as well as close-textual analyses can help with this needed form Al-Nakba consciousness-raising.

Even the attempted suppression of some "catastrophe" memories has backfired and aided with Al-Nakba consciousness-raising. As Gutman explained in 2015 there was a great of irony that was witnessed in Israeli society in the aftermath of the passage of "the Nakba Law," because the bans on Nakba commemoration during Israeli Independence Day didn't block or decrease Israeli public interest in this topic. Instead, the Israeli state's reaction to the Palestinian Arab activism "helped disseminate it widely among Jewish-Israelis."[97]

This gets riskier when Palestinians and others try to make claims about the evolutionary nature of Zionist violence as they tether together the violence of 1948 and the destruction of Gaza during Operation Protective Edge (OPE). Journalists and others who covered OPE occasionally linked the suffering of different generations when they recalled how the relatives of those who were thrown out of their homes in 1948 have been there in refugee camps for decades. The loss of more than 2000 lives, as well as the injury of 10,000 more during OPE, is regarded by many Palestinians and other Arabs as simply one small part of an ongoing struggle.

Again, I am not arguing that we can avoid the instrumental usage of the *epistemes* that go into the production of some major state *dispositif*. As Derek Gregory observed in his *Colonial Present*, Israeli historical narratives have tried to supplement their victories on the battlefields with monolithic control of a supposed accurate "history" that is in "always plural, always contested, and shot through with multiple temporalities and spatialities."[98]

Given this plurality, it will not be easy to talk about potential indigenocides in Palestinian contexts. The transgenerational revival of the arguments that were produced by the Palmah generation has now become ideological weapons for those who wish to respond to allegations that are made about contemporary abuse of power. In an interview that Shimon Peres, the former President of Israel, gave on Israel's Independence Day in 2013, he used a version of what Avi Shlaim calls the "old" or "conventional" Zionist account of 1948:

> I remember how it all began. The whole state of Israel is a millimeter of the whole Middle East. A statistical error, barren and disappointing land, swamps in the north, desert in the south, two lakes, one dead and an overrated river. No natural resource apart from malaria. There was nothing here. And we now have the best agriculture in the world? This is a miracle: a land built by people.[99]

This conveniently elided the ways that British colonizers during the mandate years simply assumed that they had the power, and the right, to decide who should receive which parcels of Middle Eastern lands. Based in part on what they had learned in Sunday school, British colonizers mapped out "partition" plans that would be used to hand over the best lands for Zionists in the Yishuv.

Talk of mastering Israel pasts, or acknowledging some colonial genocides, like Al Nakba, become forlorn hopes when confronting this type of hagiography.

Notes

1. Although a few writers today comment on the indigenocide or the genocide of the Palestinians during Al-Nakba, Yehoshafat Harkabi, an Israeli author, used the term "politicide" as an alternative way of explaining how the Arabs were trying to prevent the formation of the State of Israel. See

Yohoshafat Harkabi, *Arab Attitudes to Israel*, translated by Misha Louvish (Jerusalem: Jerusalem Israel Universities Press, 1972), 37–38.

2. Haifa Rashed, Damien Short, and John Docker, "Nakba Memoricide: Genocide Studies and the Zionist/Israeli Genocide of Palestine," *Holy Land Studies* 13, no. 1 (2014): 1–23.
3. Nur Masalha, *The Bible and Zionism: Invented Tradition, Archaeology and Post-Colonialism in Israeli-Palestine* (London: Zed Books, 2007), 1. See also Nur Masalha, *The Palestinian Nakba: Decolonizing History, Narrating the Subaltern, Reclaiming Memory* (London: Zed Books 2012).
4. Ilan Pappé, *The Ethnic Cleansing of Palestine* (New York: Taylor and Francis, 2007).
5. Sari Hanafi, "Explaining Spacio-cide in the Palestinian Territory: Colonization, Separation, and State of Exception," *Current Sociology* 6, no. 2 (2012): 190–205.
6. Rashed, Short, and Docker don't mind extending the definitional work of Raphaël Lempkin as they argue that many Holocaust and genocide scholars are fearful and submissive when confronted with the possibility that Zionist Israel could be a "genocidal settler colonial state." Rashed, Short, and Docker, "Nakba Memoricide," 1.
7. For trenchant critiques of this Nakba denialism see Eitan Bronstein, "The Nakba: Something That Did Not Occur," *Zochrot*, last modified August, 2009, https://www.zochrot.org/en/article/50644; Gideon Levy, "There Won't Be Peace Until Israel Accepts Responsibility for the Nakba," *Ha'aretz*, last modified September 22, 2016, https://www.haaretz.com/opinion/.premium-there-won-t-be-peace-until-israel-accepts-responsibility-for-the-nakba-1.5440683; Rami Younis, "When Will the Israeli Left Accept the Occupation Started in '48, not '67," *+972*, last modified June 6, 2017, https://972mag.com/when-will-the-israeli-left-accept-the-occupation-started-in-48-not-67/127911/
8. Masalha, *The Palestinian Nakba*.
9. Jamal Zahalka, "Knesset Approves Nakba Law," *Israel National News*, last modified March 23, 2011, http://www.israelnationalnews.com/News/News.aspx/143069
10. See, for example, Nicola Perugini, "Settler colonial Inversions: Israel's 'Disengagement' and the Gush Katif 'Museum of Expulsion' in Jerusalem," *Settler Colonial Studies* 9 no. 1 (October 2018): 41–58.
11. Henning Melber, "Genocide Matters: Negotiating a Namibian-German Past in the Present," *Stichprobem* 17, no. 33 (2017): 1–24, https://stichproben.univie.ac.at/fileadmin/user_upload/p_stichproben/Artikel/Nummer33/01_Article_Melber_Genocide_Namibia_draft_FINAL.pdf
12. Bashir Bashir and Rachel Busbridge, "The Politics of Decolonisation and Bi-Nationalism in Israel/Palestine," *Political Studies* (2018): 1–18 6.

13. Liam Stack, "No Google Says, It Did Not Delete 'Palestine' From Maps," *The New York Times*, last modified August 12, 2016, https://www.nytimes.com/2016/08/12/world/middleeast/google-palestine.html
14. Michael Rothberg, *Multidirectional Memory: Remembering the Holocaust in the Age of Decolonization* (Redwood City, CA: Stanford University Press, 2009).
15. Edward Said, *The End of the Peace Process: Oslo and After* (New York: Vintage, 2001), 208.
16. Ian Black, "1948 No Catastrophe Says Israel, as Term Nakba Banned from Arab Children's Textbooks," *The Guardian*, last modified July 22, 2009, paragraph 6, https://www.theguardian.com/world/2009/jul/22/israel-remove-nakba-from-textbooks
17. For one of the best overviews of the role that politics plays in the formation of these Israeli and Palestinian archives see Ann Laura Stoler, "On Archiving As Dissensus," *Comparative Studies of South Asia, Africa and the Middle East* 38, no. 1 (2018): 43–56.
18. Ian Black, "1948," paragraphs 1–2.
19. Ibid., paragraph 4.
20. Ibid., paragraph 11.
21. Ibid., paragraph 8.
22. Ilan Pappé, "The 1948 Ethnic Cleansing of Palestine," *Journal of Palestine Studies* 36, no. 1 (Autumn, 2006): 6–20, 8.
23. Benny Morris, "The New Historiography: Israel Confronts Its Past," *Tikkun* 3, no. 6 (November/December 1988): 19–23, 99–102. During these earlier phases Morris was willing to make claims about how traditional Israeli historians who studied Operation Dani, and the occupation of Palestinian towns like Lydda, "called the affair a 'rebellion' in order to justify the subsequent slaughter." "The New Historiography," 19. In that same essay in *Tikkun* he went on to accuse "Israeli historians in the 1950s, 1960s, and 1970s" of being "less than honest in their treatment of the Lydda-Ramle episode" 19.
24. Morris, "The New Historiography," 103.
25. Some, however, argue that there was no massacre. See Eliezer Tauber, "Deir Yassin: There Was No Massacre," *The Times of Israel*, last modified May 28, 2018, https://blogs.timesofisrael.com/deir-yassin-the-end-of-a-myth/
26. See, for example, Edwin Black, "Why International Farhud Day Stymies Invented Palestinian History," *Jewish Journal*, last modified May 30, 2018, https://jewishjournal.com/opinion/234614/international-farhud-day-stymies-invented-palestinian-history/

27. See, for example, Nur Masalha, *Expulsion of the Palestinians: The Concept of 'Transfer' in Zionist Political Thought, 1882–1948* (Washington, D.C.: Institute for Palestinian Studies, 1992).
28. Benny Morris, "The Historiography of Deir Yassin," *The Journal of Israeli History* 24, no. 1 (March 2006): 79–107, 100.
29. Ibid.
30. Pappé *The Ethnic Cleansing.*
31. Jacques Derrida, "Archive Fever: A Freudian Impression," *Diacritics* 25, no. 2 (Summer, 1995): 9–65.
32. Morris, "The Historiography," 100.
33. Ibid., 100–101.
34. See Stoler, "On Archiving As Dissensus."
35. John Docker, "Reconceptualising Settler-Colonialism and Genocide with Special Reference to Palestine, Sri Lanka and Australia: Reflections on Damien Short's Redefining Genocide: Settler Colonialism, Social Death and Ecocide," *Journal of Holy Land and Palestine Studies* 16, no. 1 (2017): 37.
36. For helpful background on Srebrenica see David Rohde, "Why Did Ratko Mladic Commit Genocide Against Bosnia's Muslims?" *The New Yorker*, last modified November 26, 2017, https://www.newyorker.com/news/news-desk/why-did-ratko-mladic-commit-genocide-against-bosnias-muslims
37. See, for example, Daniel Blatman, "Yes, Benny Morris, Israel Did Perpetrate Ethnic Cleansing in 1948," *Ha'aretz*, last modified October 15, 2016, https://www.haaretz.com/opinion/.premium-yes-benny-morris-it-was-ethnic-cleansing-in-1948-1.5449636
38. Avi Shlaim, "The Debate About 1948," *International Journal of Middle East Studies* 27 (1995): 287–304, 287.
39. Ibid.
40. Ibid., 287–288.
41. Ibid., 287.
42. Ilan Pappé, "The Tantura Case in Israel: The Katz Research and Trial," *Journal of Palestine Studies* 30, no. 3 (Spring 2001): 19–39.
43. Shabtai Teveth, "Charging Israel with Original Sin," *Commentary*, September 1, 1989, https://www.commentarymagazine.com/articles/charging-israel-with-original-sin/
44. Ibid., 100.
45. For more on *parrhesia* see Michel Foucault, *Fearless Speech*, edited by Joseph Pearson (Los Angeles: Semiotext(e), 2001).
46. Shlaim, "The Debate about 1948," 287.
47. Anaheed Al-Hardan, "Al-Nakbah in Arab Thought: The Transformation of a Concept," *Comparative Studies of South Asia, Africa and the Middle East* 35, no. 3 (2015): 622–638.

48. Grace Wermenbol, "Preserving the Past, Mobilizing the Past: The Nakba As a Prospective Media Realm," *Arab Media and Society* 25 (Winter/Spring 2018): 51–89.
49. Patrick Wolfe, "Settler Colonialism and the Elimination of the Native," *Journal of Genocide Research* 8, no. 4 (2006): 387–409.
50. Al-Hardan, "Al-Nakbah in Arab Thought," 635.
51. Wermenbol, "Preserving the Past," 51–67.
52. Morris, "The New Historiography," 100.
53. For potentially explosive ways of discussing the "invention" of Israel or nation-states see Shlomo Sand, *The Invention of the Jewish People*, translated by Yael Lotan (London: Verso, 2009); Keith W. Whitelam, *The Invention of Ancient Israel: The Silencing of Palestinian History* (London: Routledge, 1997).
54. Simha Flapan, *The Birth of Israel: Myths and Realities* (New York: Pantheon, 1987).
55. Benny Morris, *The Birth of the Palestinian Refugee Problem, 1947–1949* (Cambridge: Cambridge University Press, 1988).
56. Ilan Pappé, *Britain and the Arab-Israeli Conflict, 1948–51* (London: Macmillan, 1988).
57. Avi Shlaim, *Collusion Across the Jordan: King Abdullah, the Zionist Movement and the Partition of Palestine* (Oxford: Clarendon Press, 1988).
58. For a fine summary of some of the claims that have been advanced by the new Israeli historiographers see Anita Shapira and Ora Wiskind-Elper, "Politics and Collective Memory: The Debate over the 'New Historians' In Israel," *History & Memory* 7, no. 1 (Spring/Summer 1995): 9–40.
59. Mordechai Bar-On, "Review Essay: Cleansing History of Its Content: Some Critical Comments on Ilan Pappé's, *The Ethnic Cleansing of Palestine*," *The Journal of Israel History* 27, no. 2 (September 2008): 269–275, 269.
60. Ibid., 269.
61. Ibid., 270.
62. Shlaim, "The Debate About 1948," 293.
63. Ibid., 302.
64. Benny Morris, *The Birth of the Palestinian Refugee Problem Revisited* (Cambridge: Cambridge University Press, 2004), 482.
65. Saleh Abdel Jawad, "Zionist Massacres: The Creation of the Palestinian Refugee Problem in the 1948 War," in *Israel and the Palestinian Refugees*, edited by Eyal Benvenisti, Chaim Gans, and Sari Hanafi (New York: Springer, 2007), 59–127, 128.
66. Ahmad H. Sa'di, "Remembering Al-Nakba in a Time of Amnesia," *Interventions* 10, no. 3 (2008): 381–399, 382.
67. Ibid., 382.

68. Ibid., 383.
69. Jawad, "The Arab and Palestinian Narratives," 75.
70. Ibid.
71. Ibid.
72. Shapira and Wiskind-Elper, "Politics and Collective Memory," 19.
73. Ibid., 29–30.
74. Anaheed Al-Hardan, "Al-Nakbah in Arab Thought: The Transformation of a Concept," *Comparative Studies of South Asia, Africa and the Middle East* 35, no. 3 (2015): 622–638.
75. Ibid., 623.
76. Ibid.
77. For more on the expulsions and "transfers" that took place during the Nakba, see Masalha, *Expulsion of the Palestinians.*
78. Joseph Massad, "The Cultural Work of Recovering Palestine," *Boundary 2* 42, no. 4 (2015): 187–219, 203.
79. Nur Masalha, "New History, Post-Zionism and Neo-Colonialism: A Critique of the Israeli 'New Historians,'" *Holy Land Studies* 10, no. 1 (2011): 1–53, 1.
80. Nadera Shalhoub-Kevorkian, "Necropolitical Debris: The Dichotomy of Life and Death," *State Crime* 4, no. 1 (Spring 2015): 34–51, 34.
81. Walid Khalidi, "Special Feature: The Fall of Haifa Revisited," *Journal of Palestine Studies* 37, no. 3 (Spring 2008): 30–58, 30–34.
82. Rashed, Short, and Docker, "Nakba Memoricide," 1.
83. Shapira, "Politics and Collective Memory," 33.
84. For a typical example of renascent journalistic interest in Al-Nakba, see *Al Jazeera* Staff, "Al-Nakba," *Al Jazeera*, last modified May 29, 2013, http://www.aljazeera.com/programmes/specialseries/2013/05/20135612348774619.html. The four-part series on the Palestinian catastrophe chose to begin with the Napoleonic attempts to appeal to Jews who might ally themselves with the French so that they could check Britain's incursions into this region.
85. For a 1997 documentary film, that is 58 minutes long, that tries to help with consciousness-raising, see Benny Brunner and Alexandra Jansse, *Al-Nakba: The Palestinian Catastrophe 1948* (The Netherlands: Arab Film Distribution, Landmark Media Enterprises, 1997). This documentary was based on findings that came from one of Benny Morris' books.
86. Martin Shaw, "Palestine in an International Historical Perspective on Genocide," *Holy Land Studies* 9, no. 1 (2010): 1–24, 1.
87. Omer Bartov, in Martin Shaw and Omer Bartov, "Discussion: The Question of Genocide in Palestine, 1948: An Exchange Between Martin Shaw and Omer Bartov," *Journal of Genocide Research* 12, no.3/4 (2010): 243–259, 246.

88. Bartov, "Discussion: The Question of Genocide in Palestine," 246.
89. Shaw, "Discussion: The Question of Genocide in Palestine," 244.
90. Bartov, "Discussion: The Question of Genocide in Palestine," 248.
91. Ibid.
92. Anaheed Al-Hardan, "Decolonizing Research on Palestinians: Towards Critical Epistemologies and Research Practices," *Qualitative Inquiry* 20, no. 1 (2014): 61–71.
93. Ibid., 62.
94. Ibid., 69.
95. Shalhoub-Kevorkian, "Necropolitical Debris," 34.
96. Yifat Gutman, "Looking Backward to the Future: Counter-Memory As Oppositional Knowledge-Production in the Israeli-Palestinian Conflict," *Current Sociology* (2015): 1–19, 11. For related commentaries on memory work, see Ronit Lentin, *Co-Memory and Melancholia: Israel's Memorialising the Palestinian Nakba* (Manchester: Manchester University Press, 2010).
97. Gutman, "Looking Backward to the Future," 11. See also Orlando Crowcroft, "What Does Al-Nakba Day Mean for Palestinians?" *International Business Times*, last modified May 14, 2015, http://www.ibtimes.co.uk/what-does-al-nakba-day-mean-palestinians-1501356
98. Derek Gregory, *The Colonial Present* (Blackwell Publishing, 2004), xiv–xx.
99. Shimon Peres, interview with *Maariv*, April 14, 2013, quoted in Ilan Pappé, "When Israeli Denial of Palestinian Existence Becomes Genocidal," *The Electronic Intifada*, last modified April 20, 2013, paragraph 1, https://electronicintifada.net/content/when-israeli-denial-palestinian-existence-becomes-genocidal/12388

CHAPTER 4

Opening Up the "Pandora's Box" That Comes with Academic, Legal, and Public Acknowledgments of "Colonial Genocides"

Abstract In this chapter the author explains how many communities who are familiar with Holocaust arguments are often unwilling to take seriously calls for social redress for those who suffered, or continue to suffer, from the perpetration of colonial genocides. Using the metaphor of "Pandora's Box" many of those who wish to avoid discussion acknowledgments, apologies, reparations, or repatriations of human remains argue that if colonial genocides are recognized this might lead to litigation like the British settlements with former Mau Mau fighters. The author argues that these expressed anxieties do not provide sufficient warrants for closing off needed debates about colonial genocides or restorative justice for indigenous survivors.

Keywords Apologies • Pandora's Box • Reparations • Repatriation • *Vergangenheitsbewältigung*

In ancient Greek mythology, Pandora received a jar (later translated as a box) from Zeus as a wedding gift, and she was told not to open it. Overcome with curiosity, it was said that Pandora opened the box, and out flew all of the miseries of the ancient world, including disease, poverty, pain, hatred, and death.

Today, the figurations and allusions that are associated with "Pandora's Box" are often used in twenty-first-century discussions of the potential ills

M. Hasian, Jr., *Debates on Colonial Genocide in the 21st Century*,
https://doi.org/10.1007/978-3-030-21278-0_4

might befall scholars, or jurists, or societies, that take seriously the idea that "colonial genocides" ought to be either recognized or redressed. Tom Bentley, while researching the political usages of apologies in international relations, had this to say about some of the recent rationale that were being used by the Germany government officials who assiduously avoided the topic of paying reparations to former victims of German colonialization:

> Germany has been prepared to acknowledge the Herero genocide in former German south-west Africa, but at each stage German officials have ruled out reparations. It seems that political leaders of formerly colonising states are concerned about both the tricky task of facing the violent past in terms of their state's current self-image and the potential opening of a Pandora's box when it comes to reparations.[1]

Bentley went on to explain that the use of staged public apologies were oftentimes serving as opportunities to challenge "populists' notions of their nation's idyllic past and the present danger of outsiders—often from previous colonized territories," and that expressions of regret might help with "reconciliation" or more reflective textbooks, museums, and public monuments.[2]

The mass-mediated coverage of the filing of the Ovaherero and Nama reparations case against Germany would not be the only time that the phrase "Pandora' Box" would be used to express twenty-first-century anxieties. Shashi Tharoor, an Indian politician, wrote about how "imperial nostalgia" and the "messy afterlife of colonialism" was obfuscating how many British subjects were remembering and forgetting what happened during the "British India" years.[3] Tharoor argued that British museums seemed to worry about returning purloined jewels or other artefacts that were taken during "two centuries or more of colonial exploitation of far-flung lands," and they seemed to believe that "giving in" to any request to repatriate one "item" could "open Pandora's box."[4]

Transcontinental talk of reparations for activities that happened during the Holocaust or during the colonial years continues to appear in academic journalistic commentaries. Professor Jorge Castañeda, a specialist in Latin American Affairs, told *New York Times'* readers in April of 2019 that debates about colonial apologies and reparations for historical misdeeds and human rights violations tell us that the past is never dead.[5] Professor Castañeda elaborated by noting:

> [L]ast week the prime minister of Belgium apologized in Parliament for the kidnapping, deportation and forced adoption of thousands of children born to mixed-race couples in its former African colonies. National apologies for misdeeds, crimes and odious behavior are not new. The West German government of Konrad Adenauer paid billions in reparations to the state of Israel and Jewish people for Nazi crimes. Former President Jacques Chirac of France apologized for deporting thousands of Jews to Nazi death camps. The reparations debate in the United States continues.[6]

Some researchers may want to treat these topics in separate ways, but this is obviously not the way that many twenty-first-century observers wish to talk about various types of colonial incidents and restorative justice claims.

In this chapter I argue that global societies have nothing to fear from decolonizing colonial or imperial archives. In the same way that Holocaust consciousness-raising efforts have opened up scholarly debates about the Shoah, and have produced interdisciplinary public interest in the Judeocide, the acknowledgment of comparative colonial genocides could also open up productive avenues of critical inquiry.

The previous two chapters have provided illustrative examples of how the study of colonial genocide debates are not simply matters of scholarly disputation. Investigative journalists, politicians, activists, and laypersons are some of the transcontinental audiences who are unwilling to simply forget about what happened during fraught colonial years. Communities in Tasmania or Palestine or Kenya or India[7] are just a few of the global populations that are showing interest in applying some of the insights that come from Indigenous studies, international relations, ethnic studies, postcolonial studies, or interdisciplinary studies.

If "Pandora's Box" is going to be opened by those who engage in critical genocide studies, then they are not the only curious social agents who are seeking change. As I write these words writers are commenting on acknowledgments of a Congolese "genocide" and the renovation of a Belgian museum that used to be called the Royal Museum for Central Africa (RMCA).[8] Talk of the repatriation of human remains,[9] or the payment of reparations for slavery,[10] is now taking place at the same time that aggrieved communities are asking for acknowledgments of colonial atrocities or imperial abuses.

Momentum for might be called "decolonization movements" is building across generations and across continents, and more than a few are interested in changing the names of streets that were once named after conquering winners of colonial wars. Other activists work at critiquing the contexts of textbooks or removing objectionable statues found outside official governmental buildings. Still others ask that former colonial powers repatriate human remains, pay restitution, or carryout out substantive land redistribution. What is clearly taking place is a transglobal shift in the ways that academics and publics are willing to argue about contentious colonial pasts.

That said, if "decolonization" is going to be more than a metaphor,[11] and if the studies of colonial Tasmania or colonial Palestine are going to have any impact on the lives of those who once suffered from the ravages of imperial expansionism, then we need to find concrete ways of channeling these decolonizing impulses in practical directions that facilitate substantive social change.

The rest of this chapter provides readers with many different heuristic examples of how genocidal debates can lead to productive change, and I want to continue my criticism in this chapter by trying to answer this key question: if scholars and readers interested in critical genocide studies do participate in decolonizing efforts, then what types of "pasts" have to be mastered?

Answering Queries About Postcolonial Forgetfulness or the Mastering of Fraught Colonial Pasts

The German word *Vergangenheitsbewältigung* is sometimes used by interdisciplinary scholars as way of referencing some nation's or some regional community's "mastering of the past."[12] Researchers who write about the importance of transitional justice often contend that the arrival of belated criminal justice is better than no justice at all, and expressions of contrition or the payment of reparations may follow in the wake of public, academic, or legal debates about colonial genocides. Note, for example, the recent debates over the need to compensate Indonesian families for losses that were suffered during post-World War II Dutch occupation of Indonesia.[13]

National and international publics who feel compelled to respond to some indigenous requests try to find ways of acknowledging some imperial transgressions while maintaining respect for settler-colonialism or imperialism in general. Decolonization efforts have to be balanced with heritage preservation efforts. For example, some scholars can take the stance that in 1904 Lieutenant General Lothar von Trotha led thousands of troops in the battle of Hamakari (called Waterberg by Europeans), and that following the battle many Ovaherero and Nama men, women, and children were pushed into desert regions of German South West Africa. These acts can be figured in polyvalent ways. For example, rhetors or writers can argue that these violent colonial incidents are either not genocidal in nature[14] or not representative of the views of missionaries or colonizers who wanted to live in peace with indigenous Africans. Decolonizing today's Namibian histories has to factor in the heritage requests of tens of thousands of German-speakers living in Namibia, who view the *Schutztruppe* (protection forces) as valiant heroes who saved the colony of German South West Africa from rebels. More than a few resist characterizing all forms of settler colonialism as inherently problematic.

Other scholars who hear these types of claims about the individuated guilt of a single colonial leader like Lieutenant General Lothar von Trotha argue that this attempt to preserve the reputation of most imperialists or colonializers is exactly what is in need of decolonizing. As Elia Zureik explains, there were many varieties of colonialism that exhibited "different forms and structures," and this in turn impacts the ways that we evaluate what happened on the "frontiers" of places like Australia, New Zealand, South Africa, or Americas. Some of the large-scale projects of settler colonialism, Professor Zureik argues, involved the displacement or the extermination of indigenous populations, while at other times colonialism represented a more "hybrid" form of occupation and settlement. For example, note how the violence in places like "British India" looked nothing like the frontier settlement annihilations. Zureik also reminds us that those who write about the importance of complex colonial pasts need to make sure that they don't overlook the "specific features" of colonialism that were "geographically and historically contingent."[15]

Yet readers can imagine that Zureik's talk of traditional forms of settlement, "internal-colonialism," and "neo-colonialism" looks very "critical" and may not sit well with those who would not agree with his ideological stances on the conduct of the French in Algeria,[16] the British in "British India" or British—Zionist relationships during the Middle Eastern "mandate" years.

At the same time, it just this sort of academic argumentation that paves the way for all sorts of policy discussions regarding apologies, postcolonial truth commissions, repatriation of remains, reparations, and land redistribution.

Note how the type of queries that Zureik raises can be applied in myriad geopolitical contexts. For example, in Kenya there are disagreements about whether all of the former Mau or Kikuyu who were detained during the British "emergency" years in the early 1950s are going to benefit from the compensation agreements that were made in 2013 with the British authorities who wished to call a halt to some legal proceedings.[17] In Kenya former British "loyalists" who helped detain many Kikuyu more than 65 years ago are now implicated along the British settlers, and their descendants have little interest in supporting the "Mau Mau" reparations movements.[18]

The Kenyan "loyalists" of the decolonizing years provide examples of groups that might not be interested in re-reading colonial archives that would be used to valorize the rebellious activities of the "Mau Mau" that they, or their relatives, had to fight. Some groups' consciousness-raising comes at the expense of re-introducing some unsettling, and potentially traumatizing, postcolonial memories of contentious colonial pasts.

Kenyans do not speak in some monolithic voice, and they have diverse ways of responding to the transcontinental revisionist debates that are now taking place about the historical dangers associated with the Mau Mau or the reactions of twenty-first-century British citizens who expressed their fury when the United Kingdom decided to settle matters out of court.[19]

Many British citizens still take pride in the role that Britain placed in European imperial expansionism, and they see no reason to apologize for historical events that happened long ago. This insight also applies to those elite members of colonized communities who were caught between envy and admiration of the colonizers and nationalist hate for colonial oppression.[20]

Although there are no shortage of researchers who mention that most colonial and imperial practices "ended" with the post-World War II decolonization years, and while there plenty of scholars who remain convinced that Edward Said's *Orientalism* took us down the *wrong paths* in our studies of the Middle East or foreign diplomacy,[21] there are many other critical writers who suggest that the Mau Mau settlement cases, or twentieth-century South African repatriation of human remains efforts,[22] should serve as precedents for how national and international communities should cope with indigenous calls for reparations.

Again, for those who are curious and want to open that proverbial "Pandora's Box" of colonial genocide studies, even if some of restorative justice efforts end in failure,[23] and even if some of these restorative justice campaigns do not provide monetary reparations for victims, then they at least help with consciousness-raising and edification.

Those who support colonial genocide debates are convinced that twenty-first-century audiences are just beginning to see the benefits that come from deploying postcolonial lens or reading "settler studies"[24] that allow us to visualize, and to assess, the lingering influences, and afterimages, of countless imperial or colonial adventures. Why, they argue, should we forget these latest inconvenient truths, when many nations still refuse to treat Ottoman abuses of the Armenians as genocidal?

Based on the calls for colonial genocide debates that are coming from many public and legal quarters[25] I am convinced that in the coming years we will be hearing more about the Dutch colonization in Indonesia,[26] the French in Algeria, the Japanese military imperialists usage of Korean labor,[27] the Spanish in Morocco, and the British efforts in places like Cyprus,[28] Palestine, or the Caribbean.[29]

If we truly do live in an age where an increasing number of countries are hearing from indigenous communities about the need for colonial redress to help "master their pasts,"[30] then we need comparative colonial genocidal studies that highlight what needs to be remembered and what needs to be forgiven. As Caroline Elkins argued in 2013, court cases, previous research on the Kikuyu, and the opening up of imperial archives may have helped provide compensation to the Mau Mau, but "if there is any justice" in the world then the "rest of" the former British empire was "still waiting" for acknowledgments of systematic colonial violence and compensation.[31]

Following Caroline Elkins' admonition might mean revisiting the archives of colonizers who have left shards of evidence—that could be used in heterogeneous ways by critics and defenders of colonial and imperial decision-making. The archives thus become contested rhetorical terrains,[32] and it is not always easy to perform what Catherine Hall in 2018 called "reparatory history."[33]

Those who listen to critical genocide scholars need to be able to understand, and to respond to, the academic and public arguments that are circulated by those who object to all of this anti-colonial or anti-imperial polemics about the need to master any pasts. Defenders of empires do not appreciate younger generations rummaging through musty old colonial or imperial archives.[34] Critical investigators need to be aware that they may not always like what they find in those archives, and they need to be ready to counter the positions of those who may suffer from imperial "nostalgia" and other related maladies.[35]

Some avid imperial apologists can counter the arguments of those who are enamored with Edward Said's *Ornamentalism* by carrying out "Ornamentalism"[36] studies. This refers to the motivations of those traditional British Commonwealth scholars or other academics who want to write about the need for having a proper "context" when we write about bygone years, and naturally many proud patriots—especially elderly former colonizers will care about how we historicize and remember some of these events. As Guido Gryseels, the Africa Museum's director, explained to reporters before the major renovation of the Royal Museum for Central Africa, every pillar in that famous institution had a "double L" carved in the walls—monumentalizing the efforts of King Léopold II and the monarchy's support of African colonization practices. Charlotte McDonald-Gibson would write that decades "after their colonies gained independence, many European nations still grapple with—or attempt to obscure—their bloody imperial histories."[37]

Identity politics sometimes becomes one of the controversial facets of these calls for masterings of controversial pasts. Today, this manifests itself in both academic and populist responses from researchers, laypersons, or journalists who complain that some "critical" academics seem intent on creating a sense of guilt (often "white" guilt) when a more "balanced" approach would take into account both the costs and benefits of colonial or imperial oversight.[38]

The question of what to remember, and what to forget, thus becomes contested terrain for those who make contributions in variety of disciplines—including settler colonial studies, genocide studies, neo-colonial studies, security studies, diplomatic history, memory studies, international relations, conflict resolution, law, cultural anthropology, and critical sociology. Haifa Rashed, Damien Short, and John Docker, who tackle some of the most controversial of these types of studies in their analyses of genocide studies and "Nakba memoricide," take to heart Michel Foucault's suggestion that critical researchers need to *acknowledge their own political preferences* in these debates, and they do so by noting how they are willing to extend some of Raphael Lemkin's work on the "removal" of populations so that they can critique the "colonization of the area by the oppressor's own nationals."[39] Rashed, Short, and Docker take the position that conventional scholarship misses a great deal, and they complain that denialism sets in, when genocide researchers who employ positivistic or traditional historiographic methods do not attend to the "enduring and contemporary, genocidal nature of the settler colonial structural" relationships.[40]

Elia Zureik, who also extends Foucault's work on biopolitics and population management, similarly argues that researchers need to explore the connections that exist between what appear to be "two separate intellectual pursuits"—surveillance studies "on the one hand, and study of a regional ethno-national conflict that is the product of colonialism, on the other."[41]

Is it possible that twenty-first-century audiences—who feel threatened by Al Qaeda, the Taliban, ISIS, or similar groups—want to focus on the histories behind supposed the "fundamentalist" nature of this violence while they avoid grappling with the colonial or imperial origins of that same violence?

Again, academic concerns about expanding the scope of genocidal investigations have to be juxtaposed with the motivations of those who would rather spend time coping with presentist security concerns.

Yet all of these academic debates about remembering colonial pasts, and or all of this talk of preventing the recurrence of events like the Palestinian "memoricide," raises a related, but different question: What should scholars and readers do about the allegations that sharp lines need to be drawn between scholarship and polemics, law and policies, and the dangers associated with the "politicization" of colonial genocide studies?

Accepting the Politicizing of Colonial Genocide Studies and the Pursuit of Restorative or Retributive Justice

As I noted in the introduction to this book, although many interdisciplinary scholars openly complain about what they perceive to be the blurring of the mythic lines between scholarship and advocacy,[42] this is clearly not the position of many critical investigators who argue that it is finally time to be self-reflexive about the ideological nature of many types of social scientific and humanistic studies.

Why, if we care about the pursuit of restorative justice, should we shy away from politicized studies of what happened in the Congo Free State, Tasmania, Vietnam, and so on, if vocal communities are now demanding legal redress when they read about the historical roots of what happened in places like Srebrenica or Rwanda? Why allow those who profited from colonial wrongdoing to airbrush colonial histories so that few will return to the archives and write their counterhistories?

Again, are we going to police and limit what will configured as genocidal? As Catherine Hall has recently observed, there "remains much reparatory work to be done."[43]

Critical readers and their supporters can of course think of many other examples of situations where the *selective recollections* of colonial pasts can be linked to contemporary attempts to avoid this reparatory work. Most Americans seem to assiduously avoid discussing the colonial dimensions of the occupation of Hawaii, the Philippines,[44] Cuba, Puerto Rico, and so on, but there are also examples of potential "internal colonial" debates that may be revived in future twenty-first-century debates. Benjamin Madley has recently argued that scholars may be just beginning the process of "reexamining the American Genocide Debate."[45] Caroline Elkin's has defended the need for more British compensation for former colonized communities, but this might be just one of many examples of European politicization of violent colonial pasts. Even a cursory review of the World Wide Web reveals that there has been an exponential explosion of interest in revisiting Kaiser Wilhelm II's possible "genocide of the Herero" in Namibia.[46]

Is it possible that Pandora's Box is already open?

Make no mistake there are also times when national or international communities publicly or privately refuse to accept clarion calls for any acknowledgment or redress for past or contemporary colonial violence or foreign occupation. "In one ear, out the other," Turkish President Recep Tayyip Erdogan said in anticipation of having to listen to news that the European Parliament had adopted a resolution that "encouraged" Turkey to "come to terms with its past" and "to recognize the Armenian genocide."[47] When Pope Francis joined the ranks of those who said that what happened during the Ottoman-Armenian conflicts of World War I was the "first genocide" of the twentieth century, the Turkish Prime Minister claimed that the Pope was conspiring against Turkey. The Austrian parliament may have decided to recognize those same events as a "genocide," but Ankara responded by recalling its ambassador to Austria. Turkish authorities told the world that Austria's moves had "permanently damaged" the relationship between those two countries.[48]

Clearly talking and writing about genocides in general, and the selective remembering and forgetting of colonial genocides in particular, are weighty matters.

One of the questions that readers may ask has to do with the issue of whether acknowledgments or apologies can be made for imperial wrongs without having to go to court over each and every alleged colonial conflict that might be characterized as genocidal in nature. Not all genocide allegations have evidentiary or public support, and not all genocides are prioritized in the same way.

The recognition, and placement of a particular colonial or modern genocide on geopolitical horizons, depends not only on the existence of archival materials but access to public arenas and expressions of public wills.

Granted, many of these calls for acknowledging some colonial genocides or imperial atrocities fall on deaf ears. But one key question has to be: Should these calls be ignored by those who care about moral or legal redress? For example, given *realpolitik* realities there may be little chance that either Israelis or UN observers or any other group is going to enforce any "right of return" for all Palestinians in the diaspora, but that does not mean that that the Nakba should be denied, ignored, or marginalized.

Fears of rejection, potential land losses, demographic power shifts, or foreign intervention need not prevent critical scholars from speaking truth to power. The descendants of those living in the White Highlands of Kenya or on the farms of descendants of German colonizers in Namibia need not fear that they will have to give up all those lands if they choose not to sell. Negotiators involved in German-Namibian bilateral negotiators need to openly admit that worries about Ovaherero or Nama reparations have something to do with the agribusinesses of German-speaking communities in Namibia.

Some descendants of those abused Tasmanians, Congolese, Armenians, and so on still ask for reparations or other forms of restorative or retributive justice, but as noted earlier in portions of this book these efforts have met with mixed success. Note, for example, the anger of former Belgian communities who have had to hear about Léopold II's "forgotten" Congolese "Holocaust,"[49] the worries of German or Namibians who read about the alleged "Kaiser's Holocaust," or the responses of writers like Omer Bartov to allegations that the Israeli War of Independence was actually a major "catastrophe."[50]

One's mortification about colonial guilt, ability to afford compensation for wrongdoing, national identification, worries about precedents, legal powers, and other factors impact how one will respond to these calls for redress for imperial wrongdoing. But should these *realpolitik* concerns influence the morality of recognizing contested colonial pasts? Even more controversial will be situations where former victims become perpetrators.[51]

These worries, however, should not stand in the way of substantive scholarly inquiry, even in situations where writing about colonial genocides irks traditional scholars who don't want to hear about "double genocides"[52] as they continue to defend what some call "Auschwitz"- centered

Holocaust or genocides analyses. As A. Dirk Moses argues in an intriguing essay on what he calls the "apocalyptic conjuncture," for many historians and members of the public the "Holocaust is the protypical genocide," and this in turn is used to make distinctions been "real," "normal" ethnic conflicts/national wars and events that seem to have transcendent, metaphysical, or ahistorical meanings.[53]

Using Auschwitz as the violence threshold or genocidal yardstick means that politicians in many nations can follow the lead of academics who want to restrict their gazes as they focus on the Judeocide, the Armenian genocide, the Rwandan genocide, and perhaps one or two other conflicts that become part of the convention canons of orthodox scholarship. They can explicitly or implicitly be dismissive of colonial or imperial violence that is *thought to fall short of the scale* of the Holocaust. Patriotic communities, who were already predisposed to ignore calls for colonial genocidal redress, can now, with very little difficulty, help form alliances with those who want the word "genocide" to only apply to a few large-scale massacres.

Note, for example, the firestorm of controversy that arose when Caroline Elkins seemed to argue that what happened in Kenya during the 1950s' British colonial emergency years was almost genocidal in nature.[54] Her revisionist accounts of these imperial years were based on archival research and on interviews with Kikuyu survivors who told her about murders, rapes, horrid detentions, and the patrolling of villages by British troops who were intent on ridding Kenya of diseased "Mau Mau minds." Talk of "rehabilitation" and the benefits that came from exposure to missionary lessons and the "dilution" system were used to keep track of administrative successes in "de-oathing" Mau Mau "rebels."

Potential compensation for those surviving Mau Mau—who battled settlers, British troops, and loyalists Kenyans—is not going to come without debate and active consciousness-raising efforts.

The future provision of social justice will also have to involve contests over the rhetorical usages of humanitarian discourses that can be appropriated not only by aggrieved indigenous communities but by the colonizers who seek immunity or forgiveness for past wrongs. Makau Mutua, in his *Human Rights and Standards: Hegemony, Law and Politics* (2016), did his best to characterize some of heterogeneity of rights talk when he explained:

> No other discourse evokes as much public sympathy, or emotion, as does human rights, and opponents of human rights are demonized as inhumane, power hungry, or plain evil. States rarely disagree with the content of a

> particular right, but they hide behind spurious arguments to oppose compliance. Their objections to particular human rights standards are usually couched in arguments about sovereignty, self-determination, development, and the struggle against foreign domination and imperialism. Human rights are viewed as a noble ideal, and the only way to credibly confront them—without appearing negative—is by pitting them against another equally noble ideal.[55]

If Mutua is right, then we need to think of the various options that we have going forward as we debate about human rights in colonial genocide contexts. I therefore want to mention a few of the potential options as we open even more colonial archives.

I want to continue my analysis in this final chapter by critiquing some of these key restorative justice activities—the publicizing of apologias, the formation of truth commissions, the repatriation of human remains, and the payment of reparations in concrete situations.[56]

Reassessing the Roles That Colonial Apologies Might Play in Providing Redress

Obviously state officials are not the only social agents involved in what Dane Kennedy calls these "imperial history wars."[57] How can decision-makers and others acknowledge colonial or imperial wrongdoing without participating in what Professor Buruma has called the "victim Olympics"?[58]

One praxeological approach that scholars and laypersons might take would involve the promotion of real, as opposed to feigned, apologies. Tom Bentley has noted that although there is "something intriguing about the emerging twenty-first century phenomenon of states offering international apologies for their colonial transgressions," we still have few "systematic analysis of international colonial apologias."[59]

This may be because both scholars and practitioners are worried about the societal consequences of apologizing, or it may be that politicians and publics would rather not see their national colonial histories become a part of that "systematic" analysis.

Regardless, it seems as though members of the public who are not in favor of monetary reparations or radical land redistribution do not mind having their politicians, at times, publicly express regret for past colonial or imperial wrongs. Even in cases where reparations are not paid, there may be a need for the presentation of some form of state or personal apologia, that may or may not be accepted by aggrieved communities. For example, the Vatican once expressed regret for the failure of the Roman Catholic Church to prevent the Holocaust, the Japanese have argued they have already apologized for the use of "comfort women" during Korean and Chinese adventurism, the British have apologized for the lack of more aid during the Irish potato famine and the some Australians opened "sorry books" for citizens to apologize for the forced separation of Aboriginals during post-settlement years.[60]

Some scholars use the example of Japanese Prime Minister Tomiichi Murayama's "heartfelt" apology as an example of a political leader who can apologize for the "collective misdeeds" of a nation's past. In 1995 Murayama admitted that Japanese imperialists had, through their colonial rule and invasions, "caused tremendous damage and suffering to the people of many countries, particularly to those of Asian nations."[61]

As noted above, these apologies have sometimes set the stage for more demanding claims, and at other times the apology itself is treated as a substantive form of redress. Kora Andrieu, writing in *Millennium*, argued that while states have sometimes shied away from public apologies, they do not always have to lead to reparations or other forms of costly redress:

> The problem of the previous objections to state apologies, based on their link to responsibility and reparations, is that they neglect the essentially symbolic role of any apology. The recognition of past suffering and of the psychological and material legacies it has left in contemporary society may, in itself, be a form of reparation. For many victims, this symbolic recognition is more valuable than any material compensation: no price can be put on their suffering, and the attempt to 'monetarise' a mass atrocity is always morally problematic, as the debate over the restitution of Jewish goods and reparations for the Holocaust has shown. Money shifts the issue from a moral to an interest-based dimension, and thus risks raising ambiguities about the victims' motivations.[62]

This type of argument may not resonate with communities who seek monetary compensation as well as apologies—for example, some Armenian groups, Ovaherero committees, the Mau Mau—but Andrieu is making the argument that some simply want to decouple moralistic apologies from the quest for more monetary restitution.

Martha Minow has made the fascinating point that apologies involve paradoxes—no matter how sincere an apology may seem, it cannot undo what has been done and yet, in some "mysterious way and according to its own logic," that is precisely what some apologies manage to do.[63]

Apologies, however, can also be deployed for strategic reasons. In December of 2015 the International Center for Transitional Justice argued that while some apologies can be a form of reparation, in many cases "apologies are not enough as reparation to victims of serious violations."[64] Professor Marrus, in his analysis of the 2004 apologetic efforts of Heidemarie Wieczorek-Zeul in the 100th anniversary of Ovaherero uprising,[65] seems to view this as a flawed attempt at expressing official regret:

> [A German government effort to apologize for genocide failed] because of the clumsy delivery and the failure to address beforehand specific demands by the Herero authorities for both apology and compensation. And so although the German spokeswoman asked the Herero for forgiveness, she seems to have caught her listeners off guard, and had to be prompted by hecklers to utter the word "apology." The Herero chief Kuaima Rirauko seems to have been unsure exactly what to do. "I am not here to refuse your apology and admission of guilt," he observed. "There must now be dialogue to finish the unfinished business," he told a crowd of supporters.[66]

Other observers have treated Wieczorek-Zeul's remarks as an unqualified example of a major door-opening apology, but they forget that during that same 2004 public address Germany's development aid minister explicitly ruled out financial compensation for the victims' descendants.[67]

German officials, who are said to have acknowledged that what happened during the first decade of the twentieth century may have been a genocide, would still rather negotiate with Namibian governmental officials than have to deal with advocacy representatives.

After the presentation of Wieczorek-Zeul's speech there were those who viewed her apology as an example of how Germany was finally beginning the process of mastering its colonial pasts. Andrew Meldrum, writing from Pretoria in 2004, argued that Heidemarie Wieczorek-Zeul's remarks mean that "Germany," for the "first time," "apologized" for a "colonial-era genocide which killed 65,000 Herero people."[68] Yet for years after this, the Left Party and the Social Democrats in Germany got little support when they tried to draft documents for the German Bundestag that would have provided more substantive evidence of official German apologies. It took some 11 years before newspapers could confidently report that they felt that Namibians were receiving official German apologies for what happened in camps like Shark Island.

Truth Commissions, Commissions of Inquiry, and the Opening Up of Archives

Sometimes neither legal acknowledgments nor state expressions of regret will satisfy claimants or other stakeholders who believe that some "independent" truth commission, or Commission of Inquiry, needs to formed so that it can help document the ontological existence of some genocide. One possible way of coping with the pressure to acknowledge colonial or imperial wrongdoing might involve the use of specific types of investigative groups that are called "historical truth commissions." A Report of the UN Secretary General defines a truth commissions as "official, temporary, non-judicial, fact-finding bodies that investigate a pattern of abuses of human rights or humanitarian law committed over a number of years."[69]

These are commissions that usually meet for at least six months, and during that period they collect archival, victim testimonials, police or military statements, confessions, and other materials that might be helpful in piecing together what happened during some painful past when communities are not interested in paying for divisive legal proceedings. As Priscilla Hayner explains, historical truth commissions try to rhetorically craft an acceptable archival "record" of what happened that allows post-conflict generations to hear "unspeakable truths" as they confront both "state terror" or other atrocities.[70] Examples of historical truth commissions include the ones that have looked into what happened in Estonia and Latvia under Soviet and Nazi occupation,[71] and they are credited with helping "lift the lid of silence and denial from a contentious and painful period of history."[72]

Sometimes human rights activists may be searching for a way of preventing future denial of a particular genocide, and they could use truth commissions as vehicles for the prevention of denials of what Priscilla Hayner calls "spoken truths." Michael Ignatieff similarly remarked that since "the past is an argument," one of the functions of the "truth commissions, like the function of honest historians," is to "purify the argument, to narrow the range of permissible lies."[73] For example the truth commission may have members who might counter the claims of repressive governments, or sectors of the public, who not only carried out certain atrocities but stayed in power and controlled the formation of the dominant *dispositif* that contextualized those events.

The heuristic value of this type of option manifests itself when we think about how anti-apartheid activists used truth commissions as a way of preventing some South African communities from saying that they did not know about the use of torture or systematic abuses during the apartheid years.[74] As Timothy Ash explains, Professor Hayner once suggested to the US authorities that they add to their visa-ban lists of people who were found guilty of atrocities by a "well-conducted truth commission."[75]

Another famous example of going this route has to do with the 2015 distribution of the Final Report of the Truth and Reconciliation Commission of Canada. The discussion of "cultural genocide" in this commission's final report got mixed reviews, but it was viewed as an attempt to at recognize some genocidal facts of Canadian's old residential schools policies.[76] Others might have wanted to see more about "physical" or "biological" genocides in Canada, but this would not have resonated with most Canadians who had their own views regarding Canadian settler colonialism.

Contemplating Future Repatriation of Human Remains As a Form of Postcolonial Redress

Some indigenous communities have their own cultural ways of revering the dead, and requests for the repatriation of human remains that may be sent back to former colonized lands have become parts of contemporary restorative justice conversations.[77] For example, in May of 2014, Berlin's Charité hospital handed over to the Ovaherero and Nama ethnic groups who traveled to Germany three complete skeletons and 18 skulls that were identified as African remains.[78] These were some skulls (or ancestors according to Namibians) that had been collected by German ethnologists, doctors, and eugenicists who were trying to use physical anthropological studies of Ovaherero and Nama body parts as a way of verifying some of the assumptions that they were making about the positioning of Africans on Social Darwinian ladders. However, it needs to be noted that only those skulls or other remains that are said to have "difficult pasts"—documented by a text called a "provenance"—that are subject to this type of repatriation. What journalists often don't mention is that the handing of a few dozen skulls can be used to simultaneously rationalize the keeping of thousands of others.

Some might argue that repatriation of human remains, like some apologias, doesn't help those who need financial compensation, but this has everything to do with the eye of the beholder. When Henning Melber, an expert on Namibian history, was asked to comment on the significance of the return of these remains to the Ovaherero and Nama peoples he explained why it was especially an important gesture for the Namibians:

> The German side is very reluctant to recognize what happened 110 years ago as genocide. This is despite the fact that a UN report years ago that looked at the genocide of the twentieth century described the actions against the Herero and Nama in what was then called German South West Africa as the first genocide of the twentieth century. For the Namibians, it's important and literally speaking, it's the skeletons coming out of the closet. This is now the second transfer of skulls back to Namibia. The first (transfer) happened one and half years ago and it ended in a huge embarrassment because the German side was desperate to downplay the symbolic relevance of the act and avoided an official apology for the genocide. It is very interesting to see that the second transfer happened on a much lower scale.[79]

Professor Melber then speculated that part of the reason why German officials still avoided calling the 1904 Ovaherero-German war a "genocide" had to do with the possibility that "other European countries" worried about Germany setting a "precedent" that might pave the way for other calls for apologies from "other colonial powers who committed genocides all over the world in the colonial era."[80] Are European diplomats encouraging each other to avoid becoming entangled in repatriation rituals that have become privatized?

For decades the return of human remains by Europeans had already been a divisive topic among the ranks of international museum curators, private or state artists who put on exhibition displays, and others who cared about the protection of indigenous cultural artefacts. Now, however, after the international press coverage of the Charité handover of remains, these "bones of contention" also served evidentiary and religious functions that added new layers of symbolic meanings to these repatriation performances.

Reconsidering Monetary Reparations for Colonial Sins

As I have noted throughout this book, national and international coverage of colonial reparations debates bothers those who seem to assume that public acknowledgment of a genocide should suffice. During the spring of 2017, when some representatives of the Nama and Ovaherero communities announced that they were going to ask for tens of billions of dollars from Germany for the devastation that occurred in German South West Africa between 1904 and 1908 the official German response involved a refusal to admit any need for reparations. German lawyers in New York City argued that Germany had sovereign immunity, and that the US federal courts lacked the jurisdiction to even hear these colonial legal cases. Rupert Polenz, the German government's special envoy for these talks, explained to journalists that Germany viewed what happened during colonial periods as a "political and moral question" and not as a "legal question."[81] Contrast this with the public announcement by Italian prime minister Silvio Berlusconi in 2008 that the Italian people and government were going to pay some 2.5 billion pounds in reparations for 30 years of colonial rule.[82]

Italy's gesture was described as an "unprecedented act of contrition by a former European colonial power," and French President Nicolas Sarkozy suggested that other leaders needed to follow Berlusconi's example. Writers for France's *L'Expression* went even further and argued that "genocide, torture and crimes against humanity most definitely" were witnessed in colonial Algeria, signaling that at least some vocal dissident communities might advocate French payment of some type of reparations.[83] Readers will not be surprised to learn that within days of hearing about Berlusconi's efforts organizations in Eritrea, Ethiopia and Somalia were also seeking similar compensation for their suffering that was experienced under Italian colonization and occupation.

However, not all financial settlements are characterized as reparations, and some of these agreements may involve fragile, temporary decisions that may only represent short-term solution that are carefully packaged for public perusal. The negotiated Italian-Libya agreement, for example, was characterized as a "friendship" agreement, and for a time it was hailed as a move that would help improve Italian—Libyan relationships. However, by January of 2017, after all of the bombings in North Africa, some Libyans were arguing that when the Italian government reopened their embassy in Tripoli this involved "neo-colonialism."[84]

Again, critical scholars are mindful that not all supposed "mastering of pasts" involve selfless acts of consciousness-raising. In 2008, for example, when Berlusconi apologized to Libyan publics for 30 years of colonial rule, and Italy agreed to pay Libya what amounted to 2.5 billion pounds in reparations, there were issues raised of why this was linked to restrictions of migrants flows to Europe.[85] Was this done for idealistic or *realpolitik* reasons?

For decades Libyans had been arguing that Italian troops killed thousands of Libyans and drove many others out of their villages and their cities during colonial years, and it had taken some time before negotiators from the two sides reached an agreement that would provide compensation for what happened in Libya between 1911 and 1943. In a fascinating example of how material objects can be linked to potent ideological symbols—what Bruno Latour calls "dingpolitik"—part of the Berlusconi's compensation package was going to be used for the clearing of land mines that had been planted during "the Italian colonial era."[86] Portions of the compensation would be also used to pay for student grants, and for pensions of Libyan soldiers who had served with the Italians during World War II. Italian decision-makers created the impression that they cared about Libyan futures at the same time that they compensated Libyan communities for past atrocious acts.

Other parts of the Italian-Libyan agreement highlighted the building of a 1500-mile Libyan motorway north of the country that would link Libya with Egypt and Tunisia. It was said that the Italians wanted something in return, and Libya's Colonel Muammar Gaddafi promised that he would crackdown on the thousands of "illegal immigrants" who were leaving Libya and were crossing the Mediterranean as they sought a better life in Europe. This provides fascinating examples of how mastering of colonial pasts can serve presentist needs.

Critically engaged genocidal scholarship, which focuses on both ideological presences and absences, might point out Berlusconi's carefully worded missive *did not talk* about any historical Italian bombings or other problematic colonial practices. Instead, Berlusconi claimed that the money that was being sent Gaddafi's way was "a complete and moral compensation for the damage influenced on Libya by Italians during the colonial occupation."[87] To his credit Berlusconi also said that the large payment was going to help with the healing of the "deep wounds that have affected many Libyan families."[88]

As a further gesture of goodwill between the two countries Berlusconi handed over to Qaddafi the Venus of Cyrene, a Roman statue taken in 1913 by Italian troops from the ruins of the old Greek and Roman settlement of Cyrene.[89] Readers will have to decide whether they see this as a negotiated form of acceptable compromise—that uses that past for needed colonial redress—or whether this was actually a non-apologetic act, a cynical way of helping Italy ease the EU's migration or refugee "crisis."

While some critics have characterized parts of Berlusconi's deal as way of performing what Tom Bentley has called the "sorrow of empire" and the "performative contradictions of liberalism,"[90] Italy's agreements with

Libya at least provide us with an illustrative case example that underscores the point that many Libyans saw the need to recall the past—even if this meant politicizing colonial violence or potential eliding some genocidal practices. Granted, during this particular diplomatic exchange there was no detailed discussion of the Italian bombs that were dropped on Libyans, and we saw no elite or public interrogation of torture *epistemes*, but it could be argued that this was certainly better than some forms of Italian denialism. The recognition of the links that could be made between colonial practices and the traumas of those Libyan families may have been a positive step, but this needs to be juxtaposed with other parts of this diplomatic exchange that seemed to celebrate Italian colonial triumphalism.

As mentioned above, countries that might be included to apologize for colonial atrocities have worried about the door opening effect of those acts of contrition, and at other times families of survivors join those who question the material nature of reparation efforts. Susan Slymovics tells the story of how her grandmother, who survived the Auschwitz camp, long refused to file for reparations, calling it "blood money." Slymovics' relatives were not alone, for Joseph Sprinzak, who was at that time the Speaker of Israel's Knesset, openly argued that "the honor of the Jewish people precluded any acceptance of restitution from Germany even it was voluntary and spontaneously offered."[91] Yet the majority of those in the Knesset eventually voted to accept reparations from Germany as partial compensation for the Nazi perpetration of the Holocaust, and this money was used to build the State of Israel after the 1948 War of Independence.

Talk of reparations is sometimes considered to be a novel, and shameful, way of thinking about restorative justice but some contend that we need to admit that this form of redress has been around for centuries. Jeremy Sarkin contends that the "reparations by states to individuals are not new," and have existed "for at least a century."[92] Moreover, he argues that in spite of the belief that 100 years ago international law did not permit individuals to make claims directly to foreign nation-states or individuals, he argues that claims were filed, even in cases where events dating back to 150 years were granted. Sarkin references the post-World War II Holocaust cases, where Germany paid out over $100 billion to World War victims.[93] "Germany even paid claims in 1904," noted Sarkin, to "*settlers* living" in German South West Africa [my emphasis].[94]

Even a cursory review of articles circling today about reparations in Namibia puts on display how many Africans argue that racism has to be playing a major role in the derailing of their own reparations efforts. Why should so many support reparations for Holocaust victims while so few politicians appear to support Ovaherero and Nama reparations campaigns?

The Ovaherero have often tried to argue that they should receive reparations for what Rachel Anderson has called the need for "redressing colonial genocide," but in this particular case there may be some Namibian domestic issues or post-Apartheid legacies that might stand in the way of having most Namibians support these reparations cases. Anderson contends that if we look at the "socio-political history and structure of the Herero Nation" there once was a time when that nation exercised the power of a state, and that it received de facto recognition of being a state. She then uses the international laws dealing with "the third party beneficiary doctrine" to argue that the Ovaherero were the intended beneficiaries of the 1885 Berlin West Africa Convention that was attended by German delegates.[95] She uses these types of arguments to counter the positions of those who "widely supposed" that the "genocide wars waged by colonial administrators before 1948 did not violate rules of international law."[96]

What if the Ovaherero or the Nama were only some of the many African communities, inside and outside of the old "South West German" borders, who suffered during the colonial years? Are other ethnic communities in Namibia, who may have been stuck on reservations or did not participate in the fighting between 1904 and 1908, supposed to sit quietly on the sidelines and see the Ovaherero or the Nama pocket money that can now be used to buy back land from white descendants of German colonizers? A host of intersectional ethnic, class, and gender issues influence who was considered a survivor, an aggrieved descendant, or a victim.

Rachel Anderson recognized that if the Ovaherero won some of their reparations claims this might have implications that would "sweep beyond the borders of Namibia," but she welcomed this, arguing the Herero reparations efforts during the early twenty-first century "provided a voice for the silenced colonized masses annihilated throughout Africa and the world."[97] She was convinced that the international legal communities who respected international law needed to help ensure the provision of human rights for those needing redress for colonial genocides, even in cases where individual governments refused to hear calls for reparations. This would help counter the notion, mentioned by Sabelo Ndlovu-Gatsheni, that beyond "the equator there" were no "sins."[98]

However, there are some scholars who worry that paying "cash for genocide" ends up being a type of politics of compensation that can "distort historical narratives."[99] David Bargueño makes the argument that readers might have expected when he remarks that the crime of genocide did not even exist until after World War II. He opined that instead of applying some "new international morality" standard that appeared after World War II the Ovaherero were better served when they simply tried to understand Namibia's "distinct histories of colonialism, decolonization, and national reconciliation."[100] Allan Cooper, in 2007, similarly argued that if you applied today's notions of what constituted genocidal activity to all imperial or colonial contexts that fit, "there would be no end to the potential claims that could be made to remedy each genocide in history."[101]

Conclusion

Throughout this relatively short book I have defended the idea that we need more, not less, debate about colonial genocides or imperial wrongdoing. The case studies that appeared in the previous two chapters—on the Tasmanian genocide and on the Nakba in Palestine—have been used to advance the major argument that neither scholars nor members of the public can be content with the traditional, canonical ways of viewing "modern" genocides as affairs that have little in common with colonial "wars."

By drawing from the work of critical genocide scholars, Foucauldian genealogists, and other interdisciplinary researchers I have provided multiple examples of the benefits that would come if scholars and readers were willing to open up that metaphoric "Pandora's Box" of genocide investigations.

Those who are living in this "age of apology" are no longer content to forget many of the colonial genocides or imperial wrongs that have not appeared in traditional Holocaust anthologies or "modern" genocide collections. Like it or not public pressure, combined with scholarly paradigm shifts, are paving the way for more potential litigation as more and more twenty-first-century aggrieved communities want to follow the lead of the Ovaherero and Nama and argue that the German payment of reparations to Israel or individual Jewish victims of the Judeocide ought to serve as a precedent for (post)colonial reparations efforts.

Clearly not all readers will support my call for open recognition of the colonial genocides that I cover in the book, but I hope that they can see some of the strengths and weaknesses of the arguments that are coming from those who wish to police, or to quarantine, the traditional genocidal canons. Robert Melson could not help mentioning that some key genocides took place after decolonization, and he made the contentious claim that "it cannot be argued" that the "British practiced wide-scale genocide in their other colonies" outside of North American, Australian, and perhaps British India.[102] He then went on to make the typical argument that if we are going to study genocides from the time of antiquity then we have to study the "destruction of ancient Israel by Assyria, the destruction of Melos by Athens, and the destruction of Judea and Carthage by Rome."[103]

If that is the case, doesn't this mean that we should have more, not less debate, about colonial wrongdoing and imperial redress?

I mentioned earlier how many Turkish officials reacted when Pope Francis, after listing the crimes perpetrated by believers in "Nazism and Stalinism" (Cambodia, Rwanda, Burundi, Bosnia) explained how the "first" widely considered genocide of the twentieth century was the Armenian genocide. While Armenia's President, Serzh Sargsyan, welcomed the Pope's remarks, Turkey's Foreign Minister Mevlut Cavusoglu, tweeted to tell the world that "[r]eligious authorities are not the places to incite resentment and hatred with baseless allegations."[104]

Contrast this with the words of Heidemarie Wieczorek-Zeul, the German Federal Minister, who traveled to Namibia to help mark the 100 anniversary of the Herero uprising, where she talked not of the Germany apology for the Ovaherero/Nama genocide but the need for a "vision of freedom, justice, mutual respect and human rights."[105]

Heidemarie Wieczorek-Zeul's vision contained noble aspirations, but we need to recall this has everything to do with how interpretative communities define genocide or are willing to accept the consequences of using the "g" world. As Daniel Gross explains, when observers view "German's evasiveness" regarding Ovaherero or Nama claims, and when they hear legalistic arguments that "genocide wasn't yet an international crime in the early 1990s," this was "maddening" because it seemed to reflect worries that "declarations of genocide are closely followed by demands for reparations."[106]

This was indeed the case with the Holocaust, the Armenian genocide, and the Rwandan genocide. Yet were these defensible instances of "modern" genocides that warranted interventionism or legal redress that could be contrasted with less worthy cases of "colonial" genocidal "advocacy"?

I think not. Now is the time to realize that since the Nuremberg trials—when the victors wanted to discuss "biological" and "physical" genocides but not "cultural" genocides—many in the global North have avoided listening to some of the colonial genocidal claims that have come from communities in the global "South."

We cannot continue to demand that we "never forget" some modern genocides that have constituencies in the "North" while marginalizing or denying that other genocides happened to victims living in the global "South."

If we return to the Greek mythologies that swirled around tales about Pandora's Box, we need to remember that there was another element that remained in that jar or box when she tried to close that box—hope.

In the case of debates about colonial genocides those who seek restorative justice may still hope that the colonial archives can be revisited in helpful ways to provide redress for past and present victims of imperial injustices. They will need to be armed with the arguments and insights that can only come from open debate and dialogue.

Notes

1. Tom Bentley, "Should A Nation Apologise for the Crimes of Its Past?" *The Conversation*, last modified October 18, 2016, paragraph 12, https://theconversation.com/should-a-nation-apologise-for-the-crimes-of-its-past-66525. For other discussions of the opening of "Pandora's Box" in Herero and Nama reparations contexts, see Jeremy Sarkin, *Colonial Genocide and Reparations Claims in the 21st Century* (Westport, Conn.: Praeger Security International, 2009).
2. Ibid., paragraphs 14–15.
3. Shashi Tharoor, "Essay: Imperial Nostalgia," *Griffith Review*, 2017, https://griffithreview.com/articles/imperial-amnesia-messy-afterlife-of-colonialism/
4. Ibid., paragraph 14.
5. Jorge G. Castañeda, "Reparations: A Conversation Worth Having," *The New York Times*, last modified April 12, 2018, https://www.nytimes.com/2019/04/12/opinion/international-world/reparations-a-conversation-worth-having.html
6. Ibid., paragraphs 2–4.
7. Adam B. Lerner, "Understanding India's Case for Colonial Reparations," *Pacific Standard*, last modified May 23, 2017, https://psmag.com/economics/indias-case-for-reparations
8. See Ted Schultz, "Belgium's Revamped Africa Museum Faces a Dark Colonial Legacy," *Deutsche Welle*, last modified December 8, 2018, https://www.dw.com/en/belgiums-revamped-africa-museum-faces-a-dark-colonial-legacy/a-46629177

9. Some judges who get involved in these disputes over colonial violence and human remains suggest that the litigating parties seek mediated help instead of suing to get back Tasmanian or other remains. See Anne Laure Bandle, Alessandro Chechi, and Marc-André Renold, "Case 17 Tasmanian Human Remains—Tasmanian Aboriginal Centre and Natural History Museum London," *Arthemis*, March, 2012, https://plone.unige.ch/art-adr/cases-affaires/17-tasmanian-human-remains-2013-tasmanian-aboriginal-centre-and-natural-history-museum-london/case-note-17-tasmanian-human-remains
10. Kehinde Andrews, "The West's Wealth Is Based on Slavery. Reparations Should Be Paid," *The Guardian*, last modified August 28, 2017, https://www.theguardian.com/commentisfree/2017/aug/28/slavery-reparations-west-wealth-equality-world-race
11. For the argument that decolonization needs to include substantive change such as land reformation see Eve Tuck and K. Wayne Yang, "Decolonization Is Not a Metaphor," *Decolonization: Indigeneity, Education & Society* 1, no. 1 (2012): 1–40.
12. See Thomas McCarthy, "*Vergangenheitsbewältigung* in the USA: On the Politics of the Memory of Slavery," *Political Theory* 30, no. 5 (October 2002): 623–648.
13. Patrick Winn, "Dutch to Pay for 1947 Indonesia Bloodbath," *Public Radio International*, last modified September 15, 2011, https://www.pri.org/stories/2011-09-15/dutch-pay-1947-indonesia-bloodbath
14. Brigitte Lau, "Uncertain Certainties," *Mibagus* 2 (1989): 4–5, 8. Lau tried to argue that von Trotha was just trying to use psychological warfare when he announced his proclamation order that the remnants of the Ovaherero after Waterberg would not be allowed to return to the German South West African colony. She also argued that the German soldiers were so exhausted and weary and out of supplies that they could not have carried out any major organized plan for the annihilation of Overherero rebels.
15. Elia Zureik, "Colonialism, Surveillance, and Population Control," in *Surveillance and Control in Israel/Palestine: Population, Territory, and Power*, edited by Elia Zureik, David Lyon and Yasmeen Abu-Laban (London: Routledge, 2011), 3–46, 4.
16. William Gallois, "Genocide in Nineteenth Century Algeria," *Journal of Genocide Studies* 15, no. 1 (2013): 69–88.
17. Those in Kenya who felt that they were left out of previous "Mau Mau" settlements have brought their own claims and legal cases. See Katie Engelhart, "40,000 Kenyans Accuse UK of Abuse in Second Mau Mau Case," *The Guardian*, last modified October 29, 2014, http://www.theguardian.com/world/2014/oct/29/kenya-mau-mau-abuse-case

18. The anxieties of the Kenyan loyalists is referenced in Martin Plaut, "Mau Mau Settlement: The Kenyan Government's Shame," *New Statesman*, last modified June 6, 2013, https://www.newstatesman.com/world-affairs/2013/06/mau-mau-settlement-kenyan-governments-shame
19. See Daniel Branch, "The Enemy Within: Loyalists and the War Against Mau Mau in Kenya," *The Journal of African History* 48, no. 2 (2007): 291–315.
20. See, for example, critiques of Homi Bhabha's notion of hybridity. Benita Parry, "Signs of Our Times: Discussion of Homi Bhabha's *The Location Of Culture*," *Third Text* 8, no. 28/29 (1994): 5–24.
21. Some of these worries about the influence of Edward Said's work can be found in the critiques of the "post-Zionists." See Ilan Pappé, "Post-Zionist Critique on Israel and the Palestinians: Part I: The Academic Debate," *Journal of Palestine Studies* 26, no. 2 (Winter 1997): 29–41.
22. Sebastian Pampuch, "Decolonizing Museums in Europe and Africa," *Carmah*, last modified May 24, 2017, http://www.carmah.berlin/reflections/report-on-ciraj-rassools-lecture/
23. Kuzeeko Tjitemisa, "Ovaherero Lose Genocide Lawsuit in U.S.," *New Era Live*, last modified March 8, 2019, https://neweralive.na/posts/ovaherero-lose-genocide-lawsuit-in-us-rukoro-disappointed-but-will-appeal
24. For an excellent overview of some of the structural and functional features of this "settler colonialism" see Patrick Wolfe, "Settler Colonialism and the Elimination of the Native," *Journal of Genocide Research* 8, no. 4 (December 2006): 387–409.
25. For an example of a legal writer who is attuned to some of the critical approaches to law that can be used by some indigenous communities in Australia and elsewhere who are seeking restorative justice see Jennifer Balint, "The 'Mau Mau' Legal Hearings and Recognizing the Crimes of the British Colonial State: A Limited Constitutive Moment," *Critical Analysis of Law* 3, no. 2 (2016): 261–285.
26. Leonard Doyle, "Colonial Atrocities Explode Myth of Dutch Tolerance," *The Independent*, last modified May 29, 1994, https://www.independent.co.uk/news/world/colonial-atrocities-explode-myth-of-dutch-tolerance-1439153.html
27. Wooyoung Lee, "Japan to bring South Korean Court Ruling on Forced Labor to International Court," *UPI*, last modified November 8, 2018, https://www.upi.com/Japan-to-bring-South-Korean-court-ruling-on-forced-labor-to-international-court/7631541482073/. To provide an example of how some Japanese arguers respond to these forced labor allegations see Hiroaki Sato, "Japan's Colonial Rule of Korea was 'Moderate,'" *The Japan Times*, last modified June 29, 2015, https://

www.japantimes.co.jp/opinion/2015/06/29/commentary/japan-commentary/japans-colonial-rule-of-korea-was-moderate/#.XCOJRlxKhaQ

28. Helena Smith, "Cypriot Veterans Win Right to Claim Damages Over UK Torture Claims," *The Guardian*, last modified January 12, 2018, https://www.theguardian.com/world/2018/jan/12/cypriot-veterans-win-right-to-claim-damages-over-uk-torture-claims
29. See Hilary McD. Beckles, *Britain's Black Debt: Reparations for Slavery and Native Genocide* (Jamaica: University of West Indies Press, 2013); Catherine Hall, "Doing Reparatory History: Bringing "Race" and Slavery Home," *Race & Class* 60, no. 1 (2018): 3–21.
30. For examples of the links that can be made between academic research and public calls for various forms of restorative justice, see Rachel Anderson, "Redressing Colonial Genocide Under International Law: The Hereros' Cause of Action Against Germany," *California Law Review* 93, no. 4 (July 2005): 1155–1189.
31. Caroline Elkins, "Britain Has Said Sorry to the Mau Mau. The Rest of the Empire Is Still Waiting," *The Guardian*, last modified June 7, 2013, http://www.theguardian.com/commentisfree/2013/jun/06/britain-maumau-empire-waiting
32. As Ann Stoler once pointed out, colonial archives and the imperial parchments they contained were a part of a massive colonizing *dispositif* that helped with administrative rule in the colonies. "The archive," Stoler opined, "was the supreme technology of the twentieth century imperial state, a repository of codified beliefs that clustered (and bore witness to) connection between secrecy, the law, and power." Ann Laura Stoler, "Colonial Archives and the arts of Governance," *Archival Science* 2 (2002): 87–109, 87.
33. Hall, "Doing Reparatory History," 3–21.
34. See, for example, Ash Sarkar, "The Colonial Past Is Another Country. Let's Leave Boris Johnson There," *The Guardian*, last modified July 10, 2018, https://www.theguardian.com/commentisfree/2018/jul/10/past-boris-johnson-colonial-brexit-colony
35. See Patricia M. E. Lorcin, "Imperial Nostalgia: Colonial Nostalgia: Differences of Theory, Similarities of Practice?" *Historical Reflections* 39, no. 3 (December 2013): 97–111.
36. David Cannadine, *Ornamentalism: How the British Saw Their Empire* (London: Allen Lane, 2001). Cannadine argues that British colonizers had their own ways of rendering visible imperial hierarchies that were based on chivalry, ceremony, and respect for the British monarchy (95–126). This type of "ornamentalist" work has been used to counter the claims of those who complain about British "orientalism."

37. Charlotte McDonald-Gibson, "Forget King Léopold's Ghost, There Are Still Skeletons in His Closet," *Time* Magazine, September 18, 2013, http://world.time.com/2013/09/18/skeletons-in-king-leopolds-closet-colonial-era-belgian-museum-grapples-with-bloody-past/
38. See, for example, Tim Stanley, "The British Must Not Rewrite the History of the Mau Mau Revolt," *The Telegraph*, last modified June 6, 2013, http://www.telegraph.co.uk/news/worldnews/africaandindianocean/kenya/10103371/The-British-must-not-rewrite-the-history-of-the-Mau-Mau-revolt.html
39. Haifa Rashed, Damien Short, and John Docker, "Nakba Memoricide: Genocide Studies and the Zionist/Israeli Genocide of Palestine," *Holy Land Studies* 13, no. 1 (2013): 1–23, 2.
40. Rashed, Short, and Docker, "Nakba Memoricide," 15.
41. Elia Zureik, "Colonialism, Surveillance," 3.
42. See, for example, David Bargueño, "Cash for Genocide?: The Politics of Memory in the Herero Case for Reparations," *Holocaust and Genocide Studies* 26, no. 3 (Winter 2012): 394–424.
43. Hall, "Doing Reparatory History," 19.
44. For an exception, that moves in the direction of commenting on mass slaughter but shows some ambivalence about the usage of the term "genocide" in Philippine contexts, see Paul A. Kramer, *The Blood of Government: Race, Empire, the United States, and the Philippines* (Chapel Hill: University of North Carolina Press, 2006).
45. Benjamin Madley, "Reexamining the American Genocide Debate: Meaning, Historiography, and New Methods," *The American Historical Review* 120, no. 1 (2015): 98–139.
46. Jeremy Sarkin, *Germany's Genocide of the Herero: Kaiser Wilhelm II, His General, His Settlers, His Soldiers* (Cape Town: UCT Press, 2010).
47. Caleb Lauer, "For Turkey, Denying an Armenian Genocide Is a Question of Identity," *Al Jazeera*, last modified April 24, 2015, paragraph 1, http://america.aljazeera.com/articles/2015/4/24/for-turks-acknowledging-an-armenian-genocide-undermines-national-identity.html
48. Ibid., paragraph 2.
49. Some of this anger no doubt had to do with the mythologies associated with the "model" Belgian Congo. See Matthew G. Stanard, *Selling the Congo: A History of European Pro-Empire Propaganda and the Making of Belgian Imperialism* (Lincoln: University of Nebraska Press, 2012).
50. See Martin Shaw & Omer Bartov, "The Question of Genocide in Palestine, 1948: An Exchange Between Martin Shaw and Omer Bartov," *Journal of Genocide Research* 12, nos. 3/4 (2010): 243–259.
51. For academic and journalistic commentaries on the changing subject positions of bystanders, perpetrators, and victims see René Lemarchand,

Forgotten Genocides: Oblivion, Denial, and Memory (Philadelphia: University of Pennsylvania Press, 2011); Ibrahim Balkhy, "Where the Perpetrators and Victims of the Rwandan Genocide Live Side by Side," *Vice News*, last modified April 11, 2019, https://news.vice.com/en_ca/article/neajq7/where-the-perpetrators-and-victims-of-the-rwandan-genocide-live-side-by-side

52. Jonathan Freedland, "I See Why 'Double Genocide' Is a Term Lithuanians Want. But It Appalls Me," *The Guardian*, last modified September 14, 2010, https://www.theguardian.com/commentisfree/2010/sep/14/double-genocide-lithuania-holocaust-communism
53. A. Dirk Moses, "Historiographic Review: Paranoia and Partisanship: Genocide Studies, Holocaust Historiography, and the 'Apocalyptic Conjuncture,'" *The Historical Journal* 54, no. 2 (2011): 553–583.
54. An overview of the controversy that swirled about the British publication of one of Caroline Elkin's books appeared in Bernard Porter, "How Did They Get Away with It?" *The London Review of Books*, last modified March 3, 2005, https://www.lrb.co.uk/v27/n05/bernard-porter/how-did-they-get-away-with-it
55. Makau Mutua, *Human Rights and Standards: Hegemony, Law and Politics* (Albany: State University of Albany Press, 2016), 51–52.
56. Kuaima Riruako, the Paramount Chief of the Ovaherero, asked during the fall of 2006 for the return of land that was lost during the German South West Africa years. Riruako demanded that Ovaherero communities be given help as they tried to develop local infrastructures that helped with potable water, electricity, modern roads, and health facilities. Brigitte Weldlich, "Namibia: We Want Our Land Back-Hereros," *Namibian*, last modified August 15, 2006, http://allafrica.com/stories/200608150026.html
57. Dane Kennedy, "The Imperial History Wars," *Journal of British Studies* 54 (January 2015): 1–22.
58. Ian Buruma, "The Joys and Perils of Victimhood," *New York Review of Books* 46 no. 6 (April 8, 1999): 4.
59. Tom Bentley, "The Sorry of Empire: Rituals of Legitimation and the Performative Contradictions of Liberalism," *Review of International Studies* 41 (2015): 623–645, 623–624, See also Tom Bentley, *Empires of Remorse: Narrative, Postcolonialism, and Apologias for Colonial Atrocity* (London: Routledge, 2015).
60. Kora Andrieu, "'Sorry for the Genocide,': How Public Apologies Can Promote National Reconciliation," *Millennium* 38, no. 1 (2009): 3–23, 4.
61. Robert R. Weyeneth, "The Power of Apology and the Process of Historical Reconciliation," *The Public Historian* 23, no. 3 (Summer 2001): 9–38, 12.

62. Andrieu, "'Sorry for the Genocide,'" 10.
63. Martha Minow, quoted in Michael R. Marrus, "Official Apologies and the Quest for Historical Justice," *Occasional Paper*, No. 111, 2006, Centre for International Studies, 1, http://munkschool.utoronto.ca/wp-content/uploads/2013/05/2006_CGPS3_Marrus_Official_Apologies.pdf
64. Ruben Carranza, Cristián Correa, and Elena Naughton, *More than Words: Apologies as a Form of Reparation* (New York: International Center for Transitional Justice, 2015), 8. A much more detailed discussion of various strengths and weaknesses of apologies, see Roy L. Brooks, *When Sorry Isn't Enough: The Controversy over Apologies and Reparation for Human Injustice* (New York: New York University Press, 1999).
65. See Andrew Meldrum, "German Minister Says Sorry for Genocide in Namibia," *The Guardian*, last modified August 15, 2004, http://www.theguardian.com/world/2004/aug/16/germany.andrewmeldrum
66. Marrus, "Official Apologies," 31.
67. Meldrum, "German Minister Says Sorry," paragraph 4.
68. Ibid., paragraph 1.
69. Kim Pamela Stanton, *Truth Commissions and Public Inquiries: Addressing Historical Injustices in Established Democracy* (Thesis, Toronto: University of Toronto Law, 2010), 24.
70. Priscilla B. Hayner, *Unspeakable Truths: Confronting State Terror and Atrocity* (New York: Routledge, 2001). For readers who like to see formalistic dimensions of truth commissions Hayner, in *Unspeakable Truths*, lays out some of the key characteristics of this bodies: (1) truth commissions focus on the past; (2) they investigate a pattern of abuses over a period of time, rather than a specific event; (3) a truth commission is a temporary body, typically in operation for six months to two years, and completing its work with the submission of a report; (4) these commissions are officially sanctioned and empowered by the state or oppositional groups (14).
71. Eva-Clarita Onken, "The Politics of Finding Historical Truth: Reviewing Baltic History Commissions and Their Work," *Journal of Baltic Studies* 38, no. 1 (2007): 109–116.
72. Hayner, *Unspeakable Truths*, 25. For the interesting argument that there is not as much as a "cultural of denial" as we may think when it comes to some colonial genocidal pasts, see Lars Müller, "'We Need to Get Away from a Cultural of Denial'"? *Journal of Educational Media, Memory, and Society* 5, no. 1 (2013): 50–71.
73. Michael Ignatieff, "Articles of Faith," *Index on Censorship* 25, no. 5 (1996): 113.

74. Hayner, *Unspeakable Truths*, 25.
75. Timothy Garton Ash, "Preface," in Hayner, *Unspeakable Truths*, xii.
76. John Barber, "Canada's Indigenous Schools Policy Was 'Cultural Genocide,' Says Report," *The Guardian*, last modified June 2, 2015, https://www.theguardian.com/world/2015/jun/02/canada-indigenous-schools-cultural-genocide-report
77. For an excellent overview of some of these issues from curatorial standpoints, see Staff for the *Institute Fur Sozial und Kulturanthropologie*, "Forum: Human Remains in Museums and Collections. A Critical Engagement with the "Recommendations" of the German Museums Association (2013)," *Institut Fur Sozial un Kulturanthropologie*, March 16, 2017, http://www.polsoz.fu-berlin.de/ethnologie/forschung/arbeitsstellen/globale-ungleichheiten/news/hrimac.html. See especially the work of Larissa Förster who has been an active researcher studying German-Namibian repatriation and restitutional efforts.
78. Mark Caldwell, "Melber: German Apology for Namibia's Herero Atrocities Could Mean Compensation," *Deutsche Welle*, last March 5, 2014, http://www.dw.com/en/melber-german-apology-for-namibias-herero-atrocities-could-mean-compensation/a-17478125
79. Henning Melber, quoted in Caldwell, "Melber: German Apology," paragraph 2.
80. Ibid., paragraph 3.
81. Daniel Pelz, "Namibia Deliberates Suing Germany over Reparations," *Deutsche Welle*, last modified March 21, 2017, paragraph 14, http://www.dw.com/en/namibia-deliberates-suing-germany-over-reparations/a-38044661
82. Nick Pisa, "Silvio Berlusconi Apologises to Libya for Colonial Rule," *The Telegraph*, last modified September 1, 2008, http://www.telegraph.co.uk/news/worldnews/europe/italy/2658703/Silvio-Berlusconi-apologises-to-Libya-for-colonial-rule.html
83. Jeff Israely, "Italy Pays Reparations to Libya," *Time*, September 2, 2008, paragraph 8, http://content.time.com/time/world/article/0,8599,1838014,00.html
84. Federica Saini Fasanotti, "Order from Chaos: Libyans Haven't Forgotten History," *Brookings*, January 11, 2017, https://www.brookings.edu/blog/order-from-chaos/2017/01/18/libyans-havent-forgotten-history/
85. Pisa, "Silvio Berlusconi Apologises to Libya." For a chapter discussion on the Italian apologies for colonization of Libya see Tom Bentley, *Empires of Remorse*.
86. *New York Times* Staff, "Italy to Pay Libya $5 Billion," *The New York Times*, last modified August 31, 2008, paragraph 8, http://www.nytimes.com/2008/08/31/world/europe/31iht-italy.4.15774385.html?_r=0

87. Pisa, "Silvio Berlusconi Apologises," paragraphs 1–5.
88. Silvio Berlusconi, quoted in Pisa, "Berlusconi Apologises," paragraph 5.
89. *New York Times* Staff, "Italy to Pay Libya $5 Billion," paragraphs 1–8.
90. Tom Bentley, *The Sorrow of Empire*, 623–645.
91. Susan Slymovics, *How to Accept German Reparations* (Philadelphia: University of Pennsylvania Press, 2014), 3.
92. Sarkin, *Colonial Genocide and Reparations*, 22.
93. Ibid.
94. Ibid.
95. Rachel Anderson, "Redressing Colonial Genocide Under International Law: The Herero's Cause of Action Against Germany," *California Law Review* 93, no. 4 (2005): 1155, 1181.
96. Ibid., 1155.
97. Ibid., 1189.
98. Sabelo J. Ndlovu-Gatsheni, "Beyond the Equator There Are No Sins: Coloniality and Violence in Africa," *Journal of Developing Studies* 28, no. 4 (2012): 419–440.
99. Bargueño, "Cash for Genocide," 394–424.
100. Ibid., 414–415.
101. Allan D. Cooper, "Reparations for the Herero Genocide: Defining the Limits of International Litigation," *African Affairs* 106, no. 422 (2007): 118.
102. Robert Melson, "Book Review: *Empire, Colony, Genocide*," *Journal of World History* 20, no. 3 (September 2009): 463–466, 464.
103. Ibid., 464.
104. Mevlut Cavusoglu, quoted in *BB News* Staff, "Turkey Angry at Pope Francis Armenian 'Genocide,' Claim," *The BBC* News, last modified April 12, 2015, http://www.bbc.com/news/world-europe-32272604. See also Jim Yardley and Sebnem Arsu, "Pope Calls Killing of Armenians 'Genocide,' Provoking Turkish Anger," *The New York Times*, last modified April 12, 2015, http://www.nytimes.com/2015/04/13/world/europe/pope-calls-killings-of-armenians-genocide-provoking-turkish-anger.html?_r=0
105. Heidemarie Wieczorek-Zeul, "Speech by Federal Minister Heidemarie Wieczorek-Zeul at the Commemorations of the 100th Anniversary of the Suppression of the Herero Uprising, Embassy of the Federal Republic of Germany," *Windhoek Diplomacy*, last modified August 14, 2004, http://www.windhuk.diplo.de/Vertretung/windhuk/en/03/Commemorative__Years__2004__2005/Seite__Speech__2004-08-14__BMZ.html
106. Daniel A. Gross, "A Brutal Genocide in Colonial Africa Finally Gets Its Deserved Recognition," *Smithsonian.com*, October 28, 2015, http://www.smithsonianmag.com/history/brutal-genocide-colonial-africa-finally-gets-its-deserved-recognition-180957073

Index[1]

[1] Note: Page numbers followed by 'n' refer to notes.

M. Hasian, Jr., *Debates on Colonial Genocide in the 21st Century*,
https://doi.org/10.1007/978-3-030-21278-0

The manufacturer's authorised representative in the EU is Springer Nature Customer Service Centre GmbH, Europaplatz 3, 69115 Heidelberg, Germany. If you have any concerns regarding our products, please contact ProductSafety@springernature.com

Printed and bound by CPI Group (UK) Ltd, Croydon, CR0 4YY
25/09/2026
02222890-0017